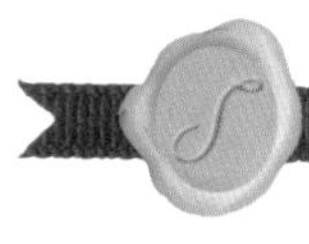

STERLING BIOGRAPHIES

SACAGAWEA

Crossing the Continent with Lewis & Clark

Emma Carlson Berne

New York / London
www.sterlingpublishing.com/kids

In memory of Ben—another explorer

STERLING and the distinctive Sterling logo are registered trademarks of Sterling Publishing Co., Inc.

Library of Congress Cataloging-in-Publication Data
Berne, Emma Carlson.
Sacagawea : crossing the continent with Lewis & Clark / by Emma Carlson Berne.
p. cm. — (Sterling biographies)
Includes bibliographical references and index.
ISBN 978-1-4027-6845-3 (hardcover) — ISBN 978-1-4027-5738-9 (pbk.) 1. Sacagawea—Juvenile literature. 2. Shoshoni women—Biography—Juvenile literature. 3. Shoshoni Indians—Biography—Juvenile literature. 4. Lewis and Clark Expedition (1804–1806)—Juvenile literature. I. Title.
F592.7.S12B47 2010
970.004'97—dc22
[B]

2009024139

Lot #: 10 9 8 7 6 5 4 3 2 1
03/10

Published by Sterling Publishing Co., Inc.
387 Park Avenue South, New York, NY 10016

Distributed in Canada by Sterling Publishing
c/o Canadian Manda Group, 165 Dufferin Street
Toronto, Ontario, Canada M6K 3H6
Distributed in the United Kingdom by GMC Distribution Services
Castle Place, 166 High Street, Lewes, East Sussex, England BN7 1XU
Distributed in Australia by Capricorn Link (Australia) Pty. Ltd.
P.O. Box 704, Windsor, NSW 2756, Australia

Printed in China

Sterling ISBN 978-1-4027-5738-9 (paperback)
ISBN 978-1-4027-6845-3 (hardcover)

Image research by Larry Schwartz

For information about custom editions, special sales, premium and corporate purchases, please contact Sterling Special Sales Department at 800-805-5489 or specialsales@sterlingpublishing.com.

Contents

Events in the Life of Sacagawea

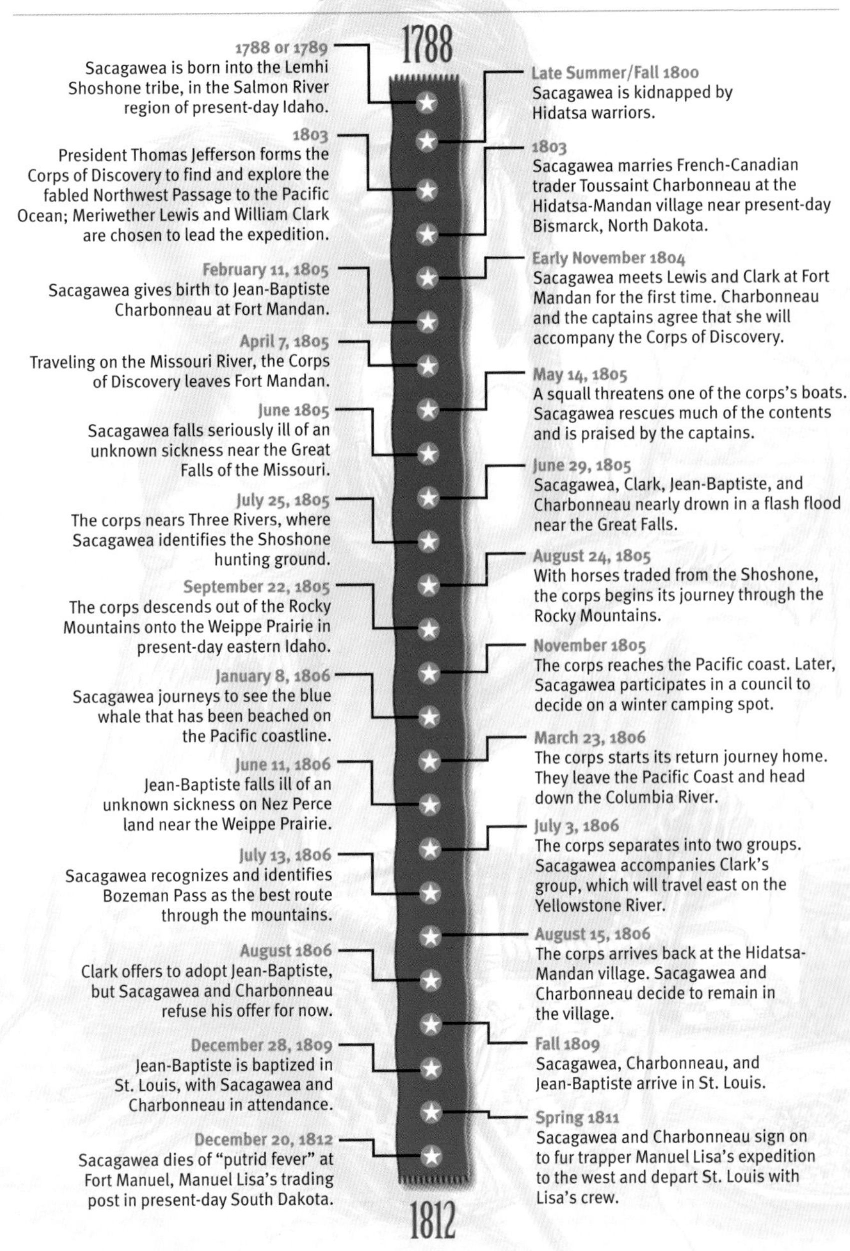

1788 or 1789
Sacagawea is born into the Lemhi Shoshone tribe, in the Salmon River region of present-day Idaho.

Late Summer/Fall 1800
Sacagawea is kidnapped by Hidatsa warriors.

1803
President Thomas Jefferson forms the Corps of Discovery to find and explore the fabled Northwest Passage to the Pacific Ocean; Meriwether Lewis and William Clark are chosen to lead the expedition.

1803
Sacagawea marries French-Canadian trader Toussaint Charbonneau at the Hidatsa-Mandan village near present-day Bismarck, North Dakota.

Early November 1804
Sacagawea meets Lewis and Clark at Fort Mandan for the first time. Charbonneau and the captains agree that she will accompany the Corps of Discovery.

February 11, 1805
Sacagawea gives birth to Jean-Baptiste Charbonneau at Fort Mandan.

April 7, 1805
Traveling on the Missouri River, the Corps of Discovery leaves Fort Mandan.

May 14, 1805
A squall threatens one of the corps's boats. Sacagawea rescues much of the contents and is praised by the captains.

June 1805
Sacagawea falls seriously ill of an unknown sickness near the Great Falls of the Missouri.

June 29, 1805
Sacagawea, Clark, Jean-Baptiste, and Charbonneau nearly drown in a flash flood near the Great Falls.

July 25, 1805
The corps nears Three Rivers, where Sacagawea identifies the Shoshone hunting ground.

August 24, 1805
With horses traded from the Shoshone, the corps begins its journey through the Rocky Mountains.

September 22, 1805
The corps descends out of the Rocky Mountains onto the Weippe Prairie in present-day eastern Idaho.

November 1805
The corps reaches the Pacific coast. Later, Sacagawea participates in a council to decide on a winter camping spot.

January 8, 1806
Sacagawea journeys to see the blue whale that has been beached on the Pacific coastline.

March 23, 1806
The corps starts its return journey home. They leave the Pacific Coast and head down the Columbia River.

June 11, 1806
Jean-Baptiste falls ill of an unknown sickness on Nez Perce land near the Weippe Prairie.

July 3, 1806
The corps separates into two groups. Sacagawea accompanies Clark's group, which will travel east on the Yellowstone River.

July 13, 1806
Sacagawea recognizes and identifies Bozeman Pass as the best route through the mountains.

August 15, 1806
The corps arrives back at the Hidatsa-Mandan village. Sacagawea and Charbonneau decide to remain in the village.

August 1806
Clark offers to adopt Jean-Baptiste, but Sacagawea and Charbonneau refuse his offer for now.

Fall 1809
Sacagawea, Charbonneau, and Jean-Baptiste arrive in St. Louis.

December 28, 1809
Jean-Baptiste is baptized in St. Louis, with Sacagawea and Charbonneau in attendance.

Spring 1811
Sacagawea and Charbonneau sign on to fur trapper Manuel Lisa's expedition to the west and depart St. Louis with Lisa's crew.

December 20, 1812
Sacagawea dies of "putrid fever" at Fort Manuel, Manuel Lisa's trading post in present-day South Dakota.

The Land of Her Birth

[The] Indian woman recognized the point of a high plain . . . which she informed us was not very distant from the summer retreat of her nation. . . .

—*Meriwether Lewis*

The Native American girl Sacagawea had been traveling up the Missouri River for four months as a member of the Corps of Discovery, an expedition led by Captains Meriwether Lewis and William Clark. They were exploring the vast uncharted land west of the Mississippi River. Sacagawea was acting as a guide and interpreter for the **corps**.

For weeks, the landscape had stretched into an indistinguishable blur of water, pine trees, and boulders. Now, though, as Sacagawea trudged along the riverbank, she suddenly recognized this land! There was Beaverhead Rock, a huge limestone outcropping rearing its head before them. Sacagawea grabbed Lewis's arm and gestured—they were nearing the land of her native tribe, the Lemhi Shoshone! She had not seen her family since her kidnapping several years before, when she was only ten. Now, Sacagawea knew she had returned to the place of her birth.

While in the service of the Corps of Discovery and with her baby strapped to her back, Sacagawea had endured unimaginable dangers—storms, capsized boats, serious illness, and a near drowning. We know little about her feelings and desires during this time, since she left no records of her own. But we do know that Lewis and Clark never would have succeeded on their journey without her.

CHAPTER 1

A Shoshone Girl, a Hidatsa Captive

[She] assures us that we shall either find her people on this river or on the river immediately west of [its] source.

—Meriwether Lewis

The land near the Salmon River, in present-day Idaho, is rugged and staggeringly beautiful. In this place of long snowy winters and short, treasured summers, the Native American girl Sacagawea was born in 1788 or 1789. "Sacagawea" probably means "Bird Woman," although some believe her name means "Boat Launcher" or "Boat Pusher."

A present-day photograph of the Salmon River shows the beauty of the area as Sacagawea may have seen it.

Sacagawea was a member of the Shoshone tribe. Pictured here is an undated image of a Shoshone father and son in Idaho.

Her tribe, the Shoshone, was very large. Groups of Shoshone, called bands, spread across what is today Utah, Wyoming, Idaho, and Nevada. Today, we know Sacagawea's own particular band as the Lemhi Shoshone. "Lemhi" was a name given to the band in 1855 by Mormon settlers.

An Oral History

Sacagawea lived in a time of exploration and change. For thousands of years, Native American tribes lived, fought, and hunted throughout the vast midsection of the United States. By the beginning of the nineteenth century, white traders and explorers were beginning to push into the young nation's interior, bringing communication and trade. White settlers also brought

The Names of Sacagawea

White explorers and settlers often struggled with what were to them long and complex Native American words. Sacagawea's own name was no exception. Lewis and Clark were very bad spellers, despite their education. They wrote her name down **phonetically**, but they were constantly spelling it different ways. At one point, Clark spelled it "Sahcargahweah."

Another version came about when a member of the expedition, Nicholas Biddle, wrote a narrative of the journey and spelled her name "Sacajawea." Many members of the Shoshone tribe still spell her name this way today, stating that "Sacajawea" is a Shoshone word and means "Boat Pusher."

In 1910, the Bureau of American Ethnology, which organized anthropological research in the United States, decided that since the Hidatsa language does not have a "j" sound and Sacagawea's name had been spelled with a "g" eight times in Lewis and Clark's journals, it must be spelled "Sacagawea"—pronounced "Sack-ah-gah-way-ah." Today, government agencies, including the U.S. Board on Geographic Names and the National Park Service, use this spelling. However, the state of North Dakota insists on even further accuracy. According to the state government, a more precise spelling of the word for "Bird Woman" would be "Sakakawea."

sickness, in the form of smallpox, to the tribes, and battles between white settlers and Native Americans brought death.

Despite all of the adventures Sacagawea had throughout her life, we know only some of her actions and almost none of her thoughts and feelings. There are several reasons for this.

Fur traders were some of the first white men to deal with Native Americans. This 19th-century illustration depicts traders from the Hudson Bay Trade Shop exchanging fur from local Native Americans for goods, such as guns.

Native Americans, including the Lemhi Shoshone, had an almost entirely oral-history culture. This means that history was passed down by word of mouth, through stories and songs, rather than written on paper or depicted in drawings or paintings. Throughout most of American history, no one paid much attention to the oral histories of Native Americans. Certainly the white people who were in power just didn't think they were that important. So if there were any stories or memories of Sacagawea as a little girl from her own people, they were lost many, many years ago.

Sacagawea lived in a time of exploration and change.

Another reason so little is known about Sacagawea, and especially her early life, is that her band had never had contact

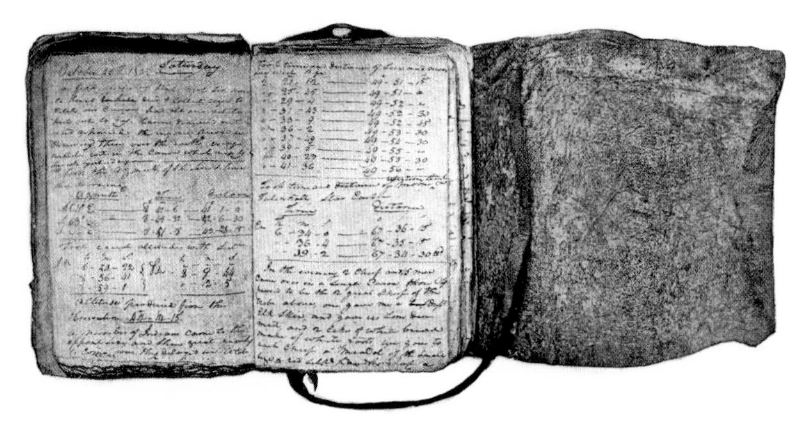

Much of what we know about Sacagawea came from the journals of Lewis and Clark. Actual pages from William Clark's journal are shown here.

with white people before the arrival of the Lewis and Clark expedition. So historians, even today, only know some details about how the Lemhi Shoshone lived, ate, worked, and hunted.

Almost everything we know of Sacagawea comes from the extensive journals that Lewis and Clark kept throughout their historic journey across the country. Neither captain, however, thought it necessary to record what a Native American woman thought or felt about events, except in very rare cases. Mostly, Lewis and Clark simply recorded what *happened* on their journey, noting the weather and surroundings, and simple actions, including those of Sacagawea.

Life of the Lemhi Shoshone

Sacagawea's Shoshone band was **seminomadic**; during the summer, they would travel over long distances, visiting various hunting grounds in search of buffalo. Animals were essential to their survival, providing meat for food; skins and tendons for clothing and shelter; and bones for needles, dishes, and other

Finding a Name

The native people of North and South America were labeled "Indians" by the explorer Christopher Columbus, who believed that he had landed in the Indies. Of course, he was wrong, but the label stuck and has been in use throughout most of American history. Today, some native people prefer the label "Native Americans," while others prefer to be called "American Indians." The Smithsonian Institution's museum of native culture is called the National Museum of the American Indian, for instance.

Shown here is an undated engraving of Christopher Columbus, the explorer who coined the term *Indian*.

Artist George Catlin captures a Comanche buffalo hunt of the 1830s. The buffalo provided food, clothing, and shelter as well as other necessary goods for Native Americans of that era.

goods. In the winter, the people would gather in their village high up in the Rocky Mountains, where the rough terrain protected them from attacks by enemy tribes. There, they would fish from the Salmon River, and hunt deer and mountain sheep for their meat and skins.

The Lemhi were a poor people—their mountain home, though beautiful, did not provide abundant food. They were kept from the more fertile valleys by better-armed enemy tribes such as the Blackfeet. Despite their poverty, the Lemhi had a reputation for raising fine horses. Over one hundred years before Lewis and Clark, during the late seventeenth century, the Lemhi had acquired horses from the Comanche tribe in the Southwest, who, in turn, had gotten horses from the Spanish ***conquistadores*** in Mexico.

Nothing is known about Sacagawea's life with her tribe, except that she had a brother and a sister. Most likely, when she was a very little girl, she would have been allowed to play games and run about the village with other children, clad in nothing at all in the summer, and warmly dressed in rabbit skins in the winter. But as soon as she was able, she would have been expected to spend her days helping her mother and other women with the activities necessary to keep them all alive.

Native American women worked extremely hard to keep the tribe well fed, clothed, and sheltered. In this 1899 photograph, two women prepare a meal over a campfire.

Native American women worked very hard. They were responsible for caring for the young children; cooking and drying meat; preparing fresh furs so that they could be used for clothing, blankets, and floor coverings; tanning skins into leather; sewing clothes, tents, and moccasins; pitching tents and making camp when traveling; taking down tents and packing horses when leaving a campsite; as well as cooking meals and gathering firewood.

Women and girls in Sacagawea's tribe were considered the property of their husbands and fathers. Men frequently had more than one wife and could trade one, or a daughter, for other valuable items, such as horses. As a baby, Sacagawea had been promised in marriage by her family to an older man. In return, her father would have received horses or mules. At around the age of thirteen or fourteen, Sacagawea would have been married to her fellow Shoshone. But she never did, because in 1800, an event occurred that changed her life forever.

Dealing with the Enemy

Every year in the summer, when the buffalo were fattest, the Lemhi saddled their horses, loaded tents onto horse-drawn **travois**, and traveled down the mountain, in what is now Montana, to Three Forks—named for the three massive streams that met at one point. It was the Lemhi Shoshone's regular summer camp, where they would stage massive buffalo hunts and spend days butchering the huge animals and drying the meat, eventually collecting enough to feed the tribe for the rest of the year.

However, the buffalo were not the only creatures in danger during trips to Three Forks. An enemy tribe, the Hidatsa, regularly stalked the Shoshone when they came down from their mountain homes into the river valley. During Sacagawea's time, Native American tribes often fought each other and conducted regular attacks on villages or camps. These battles were ways for tribes to capture valuable goods, such as horses, guns, meat—and prisoners. Warriors also demonstrated their fighting skills and power during attacks, to prove that they were more powerful than their opponents.

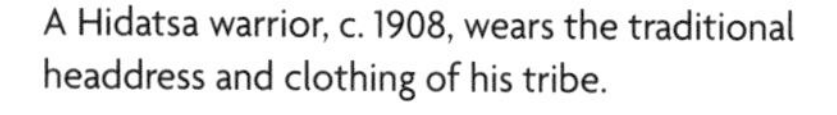

A Hidatsa warrior, c. 1908, wears the traditional headdress and clothing of his tribe.

Native Americans eventually acquired firearms for hunting as well as fighting other tribes and white settlers. This photograph from the late 19th century shows a warrior carrying a musket.

The Shoshone had been warring with the Hidatsa for a long time but knew they were no match for the other tribe. The Hidatsa had something even the fastest Shoshone horses couldn't outrun: guns. The Shoshone bows and arrows were no match for their enemy's muskets. Over the years, the Hidatsa had stolen many valuable horses from the Shoshone and had even captured women and children. The captives were taken back to the Hidatsa villages and kept as slaves, a common practice among many Native American tribes. But the Shoshone could not stay away from Three Forks—they depended on the annual buffalo hunt to feed the tribe through the winter. All they could do was to be on the lookout for Hidatsa attacks.

Kidnapped!

Sacagawea was about eleven years old in 1800, and she had probably been on many buffalo hunts. But this one was to be different. One day, while she was picking berries with some other women and children near one of the rivers, some Hidatsa on horseback crept up and surrounded them. Seeing that the Hidatsa were about to attack, the Shoshone warriors leapt onto their own horses and galloped to fight off the intruders, but the Shoshone were badly outnumbered and were forced to retreat to a brushy area about three miles away. The women and children ran behind the fleeing horses, hoping to find a place to hide. But they were not quick enough. Galloping behind them, the Hidatsa caught up and killed four women, four men, and some boys.

Sacagawea and her friend Jumping Fish raced toward the river, hoping the horses couldn't follow them. They waded into the river at a shallow spot and headed for one of the small islands scattered midstream. But they couldn't escape. The horses were too fast and splashed into the river, throwing up sheets of water with their hooves. Sacagawea and Jumping Fish were lifted onto Hidatsa saddles and carried away.

A mid-19th-century illustration depicts an Indian raid on a farm. But tribes often raided other tribes and kidnapped village members—as in the case of Sacagawea.

CHAPTER 2

Life among the Hidatsa

[Two squaws] of the Rock[y] mountains, purchased from the Indians by a frenchmen came down[.]

—Nicholas Biddle, member of the Corps of Discovery

Sacagawea and Jumping Fish were taken eastward, across the mountains, to the Hidatsa village on the Missouri River, near what is now the city of Bismarck, North Dakota. But either on the journey or at the village, Jumping Fish managed to escape and somehow made her way back to the Lemhi Shoshone. Sacagawea either could not or did not try to escape.

She was kept as a Hidatsa slave for about three years. Unlike many African American slaves of that era, Native American slaves for the most part were not treated inhumanely, but they were ranked low in the tribe hierarchy and were expected to work hard. Sacagawea probably did work that was similar to what she did at home: curing meat, cooking, making clothes, and supervising babies and little children. Over time, some slaves were released or were adopted into the tribe as family.

During her time with the Hidatsa, Sacagawea also learned to speak their language, which was different from Shoshone and a difficult one to master. In those days, each of the scores of Native American tribes spoke an entirely separate language, even those who lived close to one another. People from other tribes usually communicated using interpreters, sign language, and maps or drawings

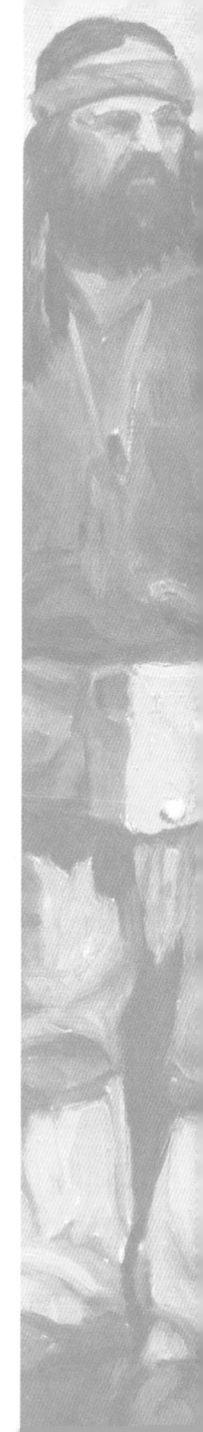

The Hidatsa Tribe

For centuries, the Hidatsa had lived in their earthen lodges at the intersection of the Missouri and Knife rivers. This central location was a trading hub and the Hidatsa became known as an advanced people. They were wealthy farmers, unlike the Shoshone. The fertile land of their home enabled them to grow valuable corn, beans, squash, and tobacco, which they traded to nomadic neighboring tribes for buffalo hides, horses, and blankets. They would then trade these items to white men from the east for guns, ammunition, knives, and beads.

An undated print shows a Hidatsa camp on the Missouri River.

scratched into the earth. Sacagawea's ability to speak both Hidatsa and Shoshone would one day earn her a ticket to one of the greatest adventures of her life.

Toussaint Charbonneau

Around the time Sacagawea reached the age of thirteen, she was given as a wife to a French fur trader named Toussaint Charbonneau. She might have been traded to him for horses, guns, or knives, or he might have won her in a gambling game.

Charbonneau was a French Canadian who had been born sometime between 1759 and 1767, near what would later become Montreal. Since about 1796, he had been living among the Hidatsa Indians and their close neighbors, the Mandan tribe. Both had villages along the Missouri River. Although some fur traders lived apart from Native Americans, Charbonneau preferred to live among them and made his home in a Hidatsa hut. He had close Native American friends and spent his life surrounded by their customs. Over time, he learned the Hidatsa language.

When Charbonneau and Sacagawea were married, she was about thirteen and he was between thirty-seven and forty-five. This may seem like a big age difference, but at the start of the nineteenth century, white and Native American girls alike usually married in their early teens, and sometimes to men much older than themselves.

When Charbonneau and Sacagawea were married, she was about thirteen and he was between thirty-seven and forty-five.

It is also important to remember that if Sacagawea had remained with her tribe, her life may not have been that much different. Her own family had

Charbonneau the Fur Trader

During the early history of America, buying and selling furs was a very big business in America. Different companies competed for the best pelts from the West to sell to big cities like St. Louis and New York, in the East. But Toussaint Charbonneau was known as a "free trader." Working on his own in this competitive field, Charbonneau would first buy goods like guns, blankets, and knives from big trading centers on **credit**, then trade them for furs from different tribes. He would then pay back his debt to the trading centers in the form of the furs he had obtained.

Like the fur traders in this 1777 engraving, Charbonneau exchanged goods like guns and blankets for the animal skins of the Indians.

A modern painting shows Toussaint Charbonneau, a French fur trader and the husband of Sacagawea.

already promised her to an older Shoshone man at the time of her birth. It is also possible that given different circumstances, Sacagawea's family would have approved of the match between Sacagawea and Charbonneau. There was no taboo in those days against a Native American girl marrying a white man. In addition, the Shoshone considered a good husband to be stable, reliable, and a competent hunter, and the French Canadian was all of those things.

A Young Wife

Sacagawea was not Charbonneau's only wife. In many Native American tribes, including both the Hidatsa and the Shoshone, men married more than one wife. Charbonneau was not Native American, of course, but he had adopted many of their ways. Around the same time as his marriage to Sacagawea, Charbonneau also married a Hidatsa girl named Otter Woman. She was even younger than Sacagawea.

There was no taboo in those days against a Native American girl marrying a white man.

Otter Woman became pregnant with Charbonneau's child very quickly, and no doubt Sacagawea thought her turn would come soon enough. Surely, she must have thought, she would live out her days here in the village with Charbonneau, bearing his children and tending his home. She had no idea, of course, just how wrong she was.

CHAPTER 3

The Corps of Discovery

[Y]our mission is to explore the Missouri river . . . as, by its course & communication with the waters of the Pacific Ocean, may offer the most direct . . . water communication across this continent . . .

— President Thomas Jefferson in a letter to Meriwether Lewis

Sacagawea prepared herself for a traditional Hidatsa life with Charbonneau. She had no way of knowing that the chain of events that would one day make her one of the most famous Native Americans in United States history had already been set in motion.

In the city of Washington, D.C., hundreds of miles from the Hidatsa villages, President Thomas Jefferson was creating a plan. From the French government, he had recently purchased a huge swath of land in the midsection of the United States. This was called the Louisiana Purchase and it encompassed 828,000 square miles. The land was almost totally unexplored and unknown to its new American owners.

President Thomas Jefferson, shown in this 1791 portrait, acquired the large region known as the Louisiana Purchase. It doubled the land area of the United States at that time.

They knew the eastern part of the continent fairly well. The western portion, accessible by the Pacific Ocean, was also known. For many years, trading ships had anchored at the mouth of the Columbia River and explored the western coast, bringing back goods and information to the East. But the vast midsection of the country was still a mystery. The U.S. government had a vague sense of the area's general geography and its Native American inhabitants—mostly from information gleaned from traders—but their overall knowledge was sketchy at best.

Jefferson knew he needed a thorough investigation of his new land. After all, the Louisiana Purchase had doubled the size of the United States. However, Jefferson was really hoping that his new purchase would contain the fabled and much sought-after Northwest Passage, a waterway that would extend from the Atlantic Ocean to the Pacific, allowing one to cross the continent entirely by water.

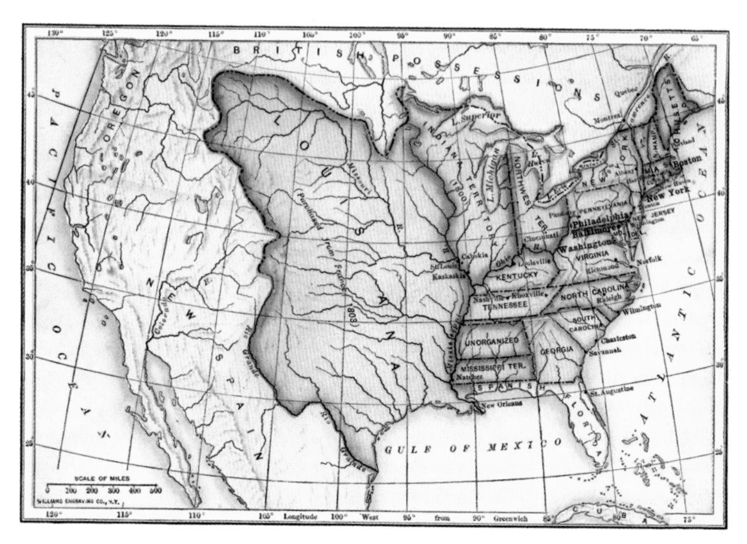

President Jefferson hoped that the Northwest Passage could be found within the newly acquired area of land called the Louisiana Purchase.

The Northwest Passage

Since the discovery of North America by Europeans, explorers had dreamed of finding the Northwest Passage. Many believed there was a series of connected rivers that stretched all the way across the continent. Such a river would open up an easy, navigable trade route—something that would be valuable beyond measure.

But the explorers and wishful thinkers of the early nineteenth century were only half right. There is a real Northwest Passage, but unfortunately, it is nowhere near the mid–United States. The Northwest Passage is located five hundred miles north of the Arctic Circle, only 1,200 miles from the North Pole. It would take another century for a Norwegian polar explorer named Roald Amundsen to first sail the ice-choked corridor starting in 1903. The journey from the Atlantic to the Pacific Ocean took him three years.

Today, the Northwest Passage is still open only to limited sea traffic. The giant icebergs and masses of sea ice make sailing the passage difficult and dangerous.

Norwegian explorer Roald Amundsen, shown in this c. 1906 photograph, was the first to discover the Northwest Passage, which ran along the Arctic Circle.

Jefferson's Corps

President Jefferson decided that what he needed was a proper exploration expedition—a Corps of Discovery. Hoping the Missouri River could possibly begin the Northwest Passage, he commissioned a group of military men to travel up the Missouri, find the point at which it joined the Columbia River in the West, and travel from there on to the Pacific.

The trickiest part would be the mountains in the West. Jefferson had heard of the Rocky Mountains, but he knew nothing about how just how large or navigable they were, where the passages might be, or, most important, whether there was a river running right through the range. He sincerely hoped there might be—for that would be the key to the Northwest Passage.

In addition to searching for the trade route, Jefferson wanted the expedition to gather information on the geography of the new land, make rudimentary maps, and conduct a survey of the Native American tribes in the area, recording their languages, customs, and manners. The corps would also chart the plants, rocks, and animals found along the way.

President Jefferson decided that what he needed was a proper exploration expedition—a Corps of Discovery.

To lead this important mission, Jefferson selected Meriwether Lewis, his twenty-nine-year-old secretary. Lewis accepted the assignment and asked William Clark, his longtime friend and former superior military officer, to be his co-captain. "The object of your mission is to explore the Missouri river, & such principal stream of it, as, by its course & communication with the waters of the Pacific Ocean, may offer the most direct & practicable water communication across this continent, for the purposes of commerce," Jefferson wrote to Lewis in a letter dated June 20, 1803.

Meriwether Lewis (left) and William Clark led the Corps of Discovery into the West.

Lewis had already served nine years in the army, and had proved himself unusually resourceful. Clark was thirty-three, and had been in the army since he was nineteen. During that time, he had developed advanced survival skills—fort-building, map-drawing, hunting, and warfare—that would be very useful on the expedition. Both captains were expected to keep detailed journals of their trip. These journals and the writings of other corps members would provide much of what we know about Sacagawea today.

Meeting the Mandan

At last, a crew was assembled. In addition to the army men both Lewis and Clark had hired, Clark brought along his personal slave, York, and Lewis brought Seaman, his large Newfoundland dog. Slowly, the group made their way from Louisville to St. Louis, and, from there, up the Missouri River to the Mandan villages near Bismarck, North Dakota. On November 2, 1804, the

Preparations Made by the Corps of Discovery

To prepare for the expedition, Jefferson sent Lewis to Philadelphia, where the young captain could take lessons in natural history, sciences, and mapmaking from the best experts in the field. Because there would be no doctors traveling with the corps, Lewis also received lessons in medicine from a well-known physician named Dr. Benjamin Rush. Lewis also wrote to Clark requesting that he be on the lookout for "good hunters, stout, healthy, unmarried men, accustomed to the woods, and capable of bearing bodily fatigue in a pretty considerable degree."

The two captains met up in Louisville, Kentucky, on October 14, 1803, where they found several more men to add to the corps. All of them were army sergeants and privates, but some also had special skills the captains thought they might need. A sergeant named Patrick Gass, for instance, was a talented carpenter and blacksmith. William Bratton was a gunsmith. Pierre Cruzatte spoke French and knew some of the sign language many Native Americans used to communicate, as did two other crew members, Francois LaBiche and George Drouillard, who was the best hunter and marksman in the corps. Cruzatte also was an excellent fiddler and promised to bring his instrument on the journey.

A modern print depicts Captain Lewis selecting men for the expedition's Corps of Discovery. Hunter George Drouillard looks on.

This undated print shows a Mandan village like the one Lewis and Clark may have encountered.

corps arrived at the Hidatsa village, where Toussaint Charbonneau and Sacagawea lived.

The Hidatsa huts were closely interspersed among the huts of the Mandan tribe. The two tribes had separate languages and some differing customs, but they lived very close together and shared many aspects of their culture. The villages contained over six thousand people.

Although there was some excitement within the villages, the arrival of the corps was not a particularly unusual event for the tribes. The Mandan and Hidatsa were used to white people. Due to their geographical position, the villages had been a trading hub for inter–Native American trade since the middle of the seventeenth century. When white traders began moving through the area, it was natural that they should choose the Mandan and Hidatsa villages as a center of the northern plains trading network.

Both the Mandan and the Hidatsa, including Charbonneau and Sacagawea, lived in large earthen huts. These huts were set closely together and had domed roofs with cottonwood crossbeams to shield snow and rain. Inside, beds made of skins and blankets were set against the walls. Each hut had a fire ring in the middle of the floor and a hole in the roof to let the smoke out. Still, the huts must have been very dim and smoky since they had no windows. The floor was dirt, covered with buffalo skins. The huts were about thirty or forty feet in diameter and most likely held several family groups. Prized dogs and horses also lived in the huts with their owners.

Building Fort Mandan

Lewis and Clark chose a site across the river from the Mandan village to spend the winter. They couldn't start on their journey when the land was covered with ice and snow. They would spend the winter among the friendly Mandan Indians, where there was plenty of food and hunting. The expedition would begin their journey to the Pacific in the coming spring of 1805, as soon as the ice broke up on the Missouri River.

Over the course of time, the two captains set about meeting the Mandan chiefs and hosted many tribe members in their tents at all hours of the day and night. Over and over, Lewis and Clark explained that Jefferson, the leader of the white people, desired peace and trade with the Indians. Everyone exchanged gifts. Lewis and Clark gave the Mandan medals with Jefferson's face

Lewis and Clark meet with the Mandan Indians in this undated illustration.

printed on them, along with beads and knives. The Mandan chiefs distributed bushels of corn and half a buffalo among the corps members, who appreciated food more than anything. Then, much to the delight of everyone, Pierre Cruzatte would play his fiddle, and some of the other corps members would dance in front of an appreciative Mandan audience.

While Lewis and Clark were forging alliances that would keep them safe from attacks and thievery during the winter, the corps members were busy building cabins. The men knew they must have better shelter than tents before the deep northern winter set in. Everyone was very glad that Patrick Gass was a member of the group: He had been a carpenter most of his life and showed the group how to build simple, strong huts. There were eight log cabins in all, each with space for sleeping and storage, all made of cottonwood trees. The cracks between the logs were stuffed with rags, grass, and mortar. So far, the Mandan and Hidatsa seemed very friendly, but the captains did not want to take any chances. A strong wooden stockade with a gate and a lock was built all around the huts. They called this temporary fortress Fort Mandan.

A modern photograph of Fort Mandan shows the stockade of the corps's winter home in 1804–1805.

CHAPTER 4

Joining the Expedition

[A] French man name[d] [Charbonneau] . . . wished to hire [on with the expedition] & informed us his two [squaws] were Snake [Shoshone] Indians.

—*William Clark*

It is easy to imagine Charbonneau crouched over the fire in his dim, smoky Hidatsa hut, making plans as news of the proposed grand expedition spread throughout the villages. He was a man who was always on the lookout for new opportunities—and new chances to increase his wealth. If he could sign on with this expedition, he could make some money and explore the trading possibilities elsewhere in the country at the same time. The trick, of course, was getting hired. But Charbonneau wasn't worried about that—he knew that Lewis and Clark would need interpreters in order to obtain something essential for their trip: horses.

Toussaint Charbonneau, depicted in this modern painting, joined the Lewis and Clark expedition as an interpreter.

Through talks with the Mandan, Hidatsa, and other visitors to the area, Lewis and Clark heard warnings of the massive Rocky Mountains to the west. The captains knew they would have to traverse these mountains, at least in part, whether or not they found a water passage. For this, they would need horses—they *had to* have horses—to carry their gear over the Rockies. But they could not bring horses with them from Fort Mandan, as they would be traveling by water all the way to the mountains. The only solution was to trade for horses once they neared the mountainous region. The Shoshone, they were told, was the tribe closest to the Rockies that had horses. For Lewis and Clark, obtaining horses from this tribe was *essential*—so much so that the success of the entire expedition weighed on this key trade.

Meeting the Captains

Toussaint Charbonneau had heard of the explorers' plans for trade with the Shoshone, so he felt confident as he strode into the captains' tent. His wife Sacagawea, he told Lewis and Clark through an interpreter (Charbonneau spoke French but no English), was a Shoshone Indian and spoke both Shoshone and Hidatsa. She could interpret for the corps once they reached the Shoshone land. If he, Charbonneau, were hired as a French-Hidatsa interpreter for the journey, he would bring Sacagawea along.

Lewis and Clark looked at each other and thought about the interpreter's proposition. Based on the languages spoken, they would need an interpretation chain: Sacagawea could translate Shoshone to Hidatsa for Charbonneau; then Charbonneau would translate Hidatsa into French for corps member Francois Labiche; then Labiche would translate French into English for the captains, who spoke no Hidatsa and no French.

Lewis and Clark agreed. They would hire Charbonneau as interpreter for the journey at the fee of twenty-five dollars a month, on the condition that he bring Sacagawea along. Twenty-five dollars was a lot of money in those days, three to five times the amount the rest of the corps was paid. What is more, the interpreters on the expedition could expect a higher status than the other men. They would sleep, for instance, in the captains' tent and eat with them at mealtimes. However, the captains warned Charbonneau, he would be expected to work along with the rest of the corps and, most importantly, obey all orders.

His wife Sacagawea, he told Lewis and Clark . . . was a Shoshone Indian and spoke both Shoshone and Hidatsa.

The men struck a deal by handshake—they would work out the written arrangement later. That night, Clark wrote in his journal, "[A] French man name[d] [Charbonneau], who Speaks the Big Belly [Hidatsa] language visit[ed] us, he wished to hire [on with the expedition] & informed us his two [squaws] were Snake [Shoshone] Indians, we [engaged] him to go on with us and take one of his wives to interpret the Snake language."

About a week later, Charbonneau brought Sacagawea to meet Lewis and Clark. She presented them with a buffalo robe she had sewn, as a gift acknowledging their new relationship. There is no record of the captains' first impressions of Sacagawea, but they would have seen a Native American girl of fifteen or sixteen, dressed in the Hidatsa style: a long dress of doeskin or sheepskin, hanging just below the knee and edged with deep fringes. The dress would have been belted just above the waist, with a tight bodice. But Sacagawea would have had to move her belt higher

Lewis and Clark's Spelling

Both of the captains' journals are meticulous, with often vivid descriptions and careful records of people and events. But their spelling seems extremely poor to modern readers. *Terms* is spelled "tirms," at one point. *Frozen* is written "frosed," *medicine* is spelled "medisan." The list is endless. Often, the captains spelled the same word half a dozen different ways throughout the course of their entries. Why were these two highly educated men such horrendous spellers? The answer is that *they weren't*. Though standardized spelling is taken for granted in our present day, it just wasn't considered as important in Lewis and Clark's time. The captains, like many educated people, often just wrote words as they sounded, without worrying about spelling them a certain way. If modern readers ever have trouble understanding terms in the journals, all they have to do is sound out the word!

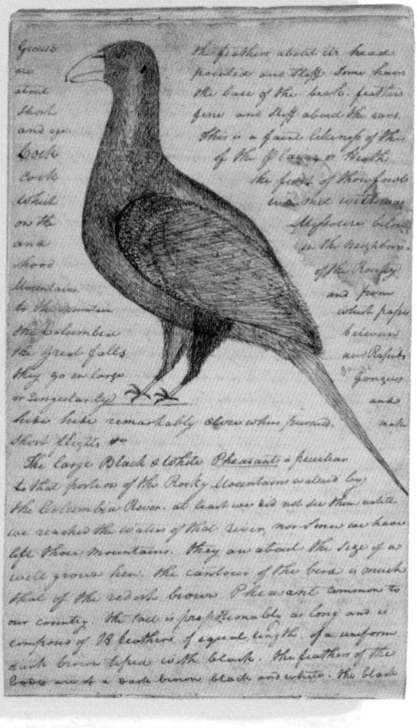
The large Black & White Pheasant is peculiar to that portion of the Rocky Mountains watered by the Columbia River. at least we did not see them untill we reached the waters of that river, nor since we have left those mountains. they are about the size of a well grown hen. the contour of the bird is much that of the redish brown Pheasant common to our country. the tail is proportionably as long and is composed of 18 feathers of equal length, of a uniform dark brown tiped with black. the feathers of the body are of a dark brown black and white. the black

A page from Clark's journal shows a drawing of a sage grouse and Lewis's description of the bird. For both captains, spelling was not an issue in their journal entries. They spelled words the way they heard them—and often used different spellings for the same word.

This modern illustration shows Lewis and Clark meeting Sacagawea for the first time. She is being introduced to them by her husband, Charbonneau.

because at the time of meeting Lewis and Clark, she was about seven months pregnant with her first child.

No one knows if Charbonneau happened to mention this tiny detail at his initial meeting with the captains or if he left it as a surprise for them, but apparently Lewis and Clark were not worried about signing on a pregnant woman. If they were concerned that she would be taking her newborn child on the transcontinental journey, they made no mention of it in their journals. Instead, they settled in for the winter, satisfied that most of the major arrangements were complete.

Winter at the Fort

And winter had certainly arrived. On December 17, 1804, the temperature dropped to a bone-chilling forty-five degrees below zero. Despite the cold, construction on Fort Mandan went forward and the stockade was completed on Christmas Day. The men celebrated with a gun salute and everyone was given a glass of brandy or whiskey. The fiddler Pierre Cruzatte, who had only one eye, played, and the men danced to his music all day long, much to the delight and amusement of their many Mandan and Hidatsa visitors. Sacagawea attended this celebration, along with Otter Woman and her little boy. The women did not dance, as that would not have been considered appropriate, but merely watched from the sidelines, seated cross-legged and wrapped warmly in blankets and buffalo robes.

By early February, stores of food were running low, so Charbonneau, Clark, and some other corps members left the relative comforts of the fort to undertake an arduous hunting trip. Sacagawea did not accompany them, of course, but she was most likely happy to stay back at the fort where she now lived, probably cooking what little meat was available, gathering firewood, and trying to stay warm. Withstanding the bitter cold, the men eventually found meat and made it back—just in time for the birth of Sacagawea and Charbonneau's child.

Corps members celebrate Christmas at Fort Mandan in this modern depiction.

CHAPTER 5

Birth and Unrest at Fort Mandan

[O]ur interpreter [Charbonneau], [determines] on not proceeding with us as an interpreter under the terms mentioned yesterday.

—William Clark

On February 11, 1805, Sacagawea went into labor. Though she was not far from the Hidatsa village, there were no other women to assist her. Perhaps the Hidatsa felt that Sacagawea had forgone that option now that she was married to Charbonneau, a white man, and living with the corps in a cabin.

Sacagawea was in a great deal of pain as she labored. This was her first child and she was very young. Lewis tried to help her but his skills with childbirth were limited, if they existed at all. Finally, another interpreter staying at the fort told Lewis to give Sacagawea pieces of a rattlesnake's rattle to eat. Lewis was skeptical, but he didn't know any other way to help with the birth of this baby. Luckily, Lewis had some rattlesnake rattle with him. He broke the rattle into little bits and fed it to the laboring teenager. Ten

Sacagawea was in a great deal of pain as she labored. This was her first child and she was very young.

minutes later, at about five o'clock in the evening, a baby boy was born.

Not knowing what to do, Lewis—at the suggestion of a fellow corpsman—fed Sacagawea a piece of a rattlesnake's rattle to help her during childbirth. In this photo, a snake's rattle can be seen sticking straight up.

His parents named him Jean-Baptiste Charbonneau, but most of the time he was called Baptiste. That night, Lewis wrote in his journal, "[A]bout five oClock this evening one of the wives of [Charbonneau] was delivered of a fine boy. [I]t is [worthy] of remark that this was the first child this woman had [borne], and as is common in such cases her labour was tedious and the pain violent."

There was now a brand-new person to take along on the expedition. Sacagawea must have known that she, and she alone, would be expected to care for the newborn on the journey. It would have been unheard of for a man, especially a white man married to a Native American girl, to help care for a baby in those days. But most likely, thoughts like these were far from Sacagawea's mind during those last frosty weeks of February. She was probably too busy nursing and mothering her new baby, who would have been wrapped tightly in soft deerskins of his very own.

Sacagawea, shown in this modern painting with Jean-Baptiste strapped to her back, took full responsibility for the safety and well-being of her baby during the rough journey.

Traditional Native American Baby Care

As a young girl, Sacagawea would have been taught some childrearing skills by her own tribe before she was kidnapped, and she was no doubt instructed by her Hidatsa family before her marriage. One traditional practice for Native American mothers living on the Plains was to pound dried buffalo dung into a soft, absorbent powder, then pack it around their babies in a thick layer, which was held in place by a blanket or skin. The layer of powder would soak up moisture from the babies, and when it was soiled, it would simply be thrown out and another layer put in place. There is a good chance that Sacagawea did this for Baptiste.

Sacagawea also would have swaddled Baptiste during the first weeks of his life by wrapping him tightly in a blanket with only his head protruding from the blanket. Swaddling was a common practice among Plains tribes and has been shown today to help babies feel snug and safe. After Baptiste was swaddled, Sacagawea would have carried him in a cradleboard—a piece of decorated wood to which the swaddled baby was held in place with leather laces. With this handy baby carrier, Sacagawea could strap Baptiste to her back and be completely mobile herself.

An undated photo shows how an Indian baby is laced to a cradleboard. Native American mothers, like Sacagawea, carried their babies strapped to their backs.

Preparing the Boats

For their part, the rest of the corps was eager to start on the journey. They had been cooped up at Fort Mandan for four months but still had to wait until the ice on the Missouri River broke up. However, spring was drawing nearer, so the captains turned their attention to readying the gear.

Earlier in the fall, the boats had been sunk in the river and allowed to freeze there, as a way of storing them. By allowing the boats to freeze underwater, the men ensured that the wood would remain swollen, keeping the vessels watertight. Now the corps began chipping the water crafts out of their icy home, replacing rotten boards, and repairing holes.

The corps would be taking two pirogues and several canoes on the journey. The pirogues were open boats, usually hollowed

As the Corps of Discovery prepared for their departure from Fort Mandan, the men also built several boats out of cottonwood trees.

Shown is a replica of a canoe that was used on the Corps of Discovery expedition.

from one log, and flatter on the bottom than canoes. They were excellent for fishing, as well as easy to paddle. Lewis and Clark's pirogues were probably about forty feet long. More important, they were stable enough that a man could stand in one and walk around without tipping it over, and since they were flat on the bottom, they were well suited to traveling rivers that could be very shallow at times. The pirogues were also large enough to carry most of the men as well as several tons of equipment. The canoes, which the men made from hollowed-out cottonwood trees, were more V-shaped on the bottom and not as stable for moving around in the water—but they would suffice for the rest of the crew.

Charbonneau's Temptation

Everything was moving along perfectly by the beginning of March. Spring was just a few weeks away and already the ice on the river was beginning to melt. It was around this time that Charbonneau made a potentially disastrous mistake.

Earlier, Charbonneau had left to visit friends at a trading post in a nearby Hidatsa village. He returned to the fort on March 7, bearing gifts he said were given to him by the North West Company—a major French fur trading company in the area.

Immediately, Lewis and Clark suspected that these items were not gifts, but bribes given to Charbonneau by two French fur trading companies: the North West Company and the Hudson's Bay Company. The captains believed that Charbonneau had been paid to somehow prevent the corps from establishing American trade relationships with tribes in the areas they were going to visit.

It was around this time that Charbonneau made a potentially disastrous mistake.

This situation was unacceptable, the captains told the Frenchman. He could not do trading of his own on the journey, and if he intended to do so, he would be excused from his post as

Members of the Hudson's Bay Company and the North West Company are shown trading with Canadian Indians in this 1873 wood engraving.

interpreter, along with his wife Sacagawea. Take the night, the captains told the blustering interpreter, and think it over.

However, what the captains did not say but which everyone, including Charbonneau, knew, was that the corps desperately needed his services, and those of Sacagawea. Perhaps hoping that Lewis and Clark were bluffing, Charbonneau decided to make some demands of his own. He told the captains the next morning that he would go with them, but he would not do guard duty, would not do any menial labor, and would not be required to obey the captains' order, and he reserved the right to leave the corps at any point in time that he desired. What is more, he wanted to bring his private trade goods with him on the journey to use for his purposes along the way.

There is no record of Lewis and Clark's reactions to this ludicrous list of demands, but one can imagine there was a certain amount of clenched-jaw discussion before the captains told the interpreter that he could get out of the camp, and take his ridiculous demands with him. Charbonneau was dismissed.

A Waiting Game

Charbonneau took Sacagawea and Baptiste and left the fort. But instead of returning to the Mandan village, he built the family a little shelter just outside of the fort walls. Then, they waited. No one knows what Sacagawea may have thought about this situation. Perhaps she was relieved not to have to make a treacherous journey with a newborn baby. On the other hand, the corps expected to pass through her homeland. Perhaps she was disappointed at being denied the chance to see her native tribe once more. Or perhaps she was too preoccupied with Baptiste to concern herself, figuring that her fate was out of her control.

Charbonneau expected that the captains, crushed at losing their valuable interpreters, would come after him, beg him to return, and promise to fulfill his list of demands. This is most likely the reason he did not take his family back to the Hidatsa village and their old hut. But he had underestimated the captains. Now that they could see what a troublemaker the Frenchman could be, they had no intentions of taking him back.

After three days, Charbonneau admitted himself beaten, and requested a meeting with Lewis and Clark. There, he apologized and formally asked to be reinstated. Surely, he thought, this groveling would be enough. But he was wrong. Lewis and Clark refused him again and told him to leave.

Furious at having humbled himself for nothing, Charbonneau stormed out, and began packing the belongings he had left at the fort. The family, he said, was moving back to the village.

However, what the captains did not say but which everyone . . . knew, was that the corps desperately needed his services, and those of Sacagawea.

By March 17, everyone involved had had a chance to cool off. Charbonneau thought that he might just make one more try, before he and Sacagawea moved for good. This time he sent a friend as an **emissary** to plead with the captains. Lewis and Clark had also had time to think over their actions. They did need the interpreter badly and he seemed repentant enough now. Perhaps they could keep him under control. They agreed to take him back, with the stipulation that he would be held to the same rules as the rest of the corps. Charbonneau agreed, perhaps reluctantly, perhaps relieved at his reinstatement. He and Sacagawea moved all their belongings back to the fort, and the next day, Charbonneau was officially signed on as a member of the corps.

In late March, the signs everyone had been waiting for arrived. The ice on the Missouri River began breaking up and the mosquitoes, unwelcome but reliable forerunners of spring, returned to torment everyone once more. For two more weeks, everyone watched as the ice, shot with cracks, splintered and shattered in the increasingly warm weather. Slowly, water appeared in pools on the ice surface. Then pieces of ice came loose and floated in the water. Finally, Lewis and Clark examined the river conditions, looked over the equipment and food supplies one last time, looked at each other, and nodded. They would leave tomorrow!

A modern photograph of the Missouri River shows chunks of ice floating down the waterway during the spring thaw. This was the same river condition the corps was waiting for to start their journey west.

CHAPTER 6

The Journey Begins

The Indian woman to whom I ascribe equal fortitude and resolution, with any person onboard at the time of the accident, caught and preserved most of the light articles which were washed overboard.

—*Meriwether Lewis*

On Sunday, April 7, 1805, at about four o'clock in the afternoon, the Corps of Discovery left Fort Mandan in six canoes and two pirogues, traveling west against the current on the Missouri River. They numbered thirty-two men, one woman, one child, and one dog—Lewis's Newfoundland, Seaman. The crew had learned to depend on each other through the long winter. As they set out, they knew the survival of one depended on the cooperation of all. This cohesiveness and willingness to work as an extended family would serve them well in the months to come.

Although Clark had indicated in his journal that they intended to take Otter Woman, Charbonneau's other wife, along on the journey, perhaps with her child, she did not go along. No one knows why. One can only speculate; perhaps Lewis and Clark rethought their decision to burden themselves with another woman and child, especially if Otter Woman did not have the language skills of Sacagawea.

As the captains checked the gear one last time and the first set of rowers took up the oars, Sacagawea settled

The Canine Member of the Corps

The most unusual member of the corps by far was Lewis's Newfoundland, Seaman. Lewis had bought the huge dog during a shopping trip in Philadelphia. Not only was Seaman taken on the trip, he was entered into the expedition's log as a member of the corps. Seaman was a type of Newfoundland called a Landseer, and these were known for being excellent swimmers. They even have fur coated with special oil to repel water, and webbed feet. Seaman rode in the canoes with the men, or walked onshore with Lewis during the day. The dog was a good hunter and provided excellent protection at night. Lewis was very attached to Seaman: Once, when a group of Native Americans stole the dog, he sent out a search party to bring him back safely. Seaman traveled the entire journey to the Pacific and returned home safely with Lewis.

Seaman was Lewis's Newfoundland dog that traveled the entire journey with the corps.

herself in one of the pirogues. She tucked Baptiste into a woven basket the captains had given her to use while they were in the boats. When they were on shore, she would carry the baby in a cradleboard on her back, but for now he was safe and snug in his little basket.

Sacagawea looked back at the Hidatsa, who were perhaps clustered on the shore. She was leaving both her kidnappers and her surrogate family. She was heading toward her native land once more—yet surely she had some feelings about leaving her new tribe. But no one that day, including Sacagawea herself, believed that she would return once she found the Shoshone.

She tucked Baptiste into a woven basket the captains had given her to use while they were in the boats.

Early Days on the River

As the days progressed, the group gradually fell into a routine they would maintain for the rest of the journey. The men rowed the boats, while Sacagawea tended her baby in one of the pirogues. Lewis and Clark had planned to both ride in the boats, too, but on the first full day, one of the canoes took on some water and ruined a bag of biscuits and a barrel of gunpowder. The captains decided that for the rest of the journey, one of them would walk onshore, along the banks of the river, and the other would ride in the canoes. This way, one of them could be on the lookout for obstacles in the river from the banks, and the other could watch from the stern of one of the boats. Sacagawea often walked onshore also, usually with Clark. With Baptiste in his cradleboard, she would gather edible plants to share with the crew at supper that night.

Whether walking on shore or riding in the pirogue, Sacagawea always had Baptiste at her side.

While journeying westward, the corps was traveling against the river current, which made rowing very difficult. Every moment was a fight to keep moving forward. When they were exhausted from paddling, they would push against the bottom with poles. When the winds were high and blowing against them, even pushing with poles wasn't enough. Then, they were forced to tie ropes to the sides of the boats, and standing onshore, tow the craft with ropes against the current. Sometimes, they would even jump into the water and push the boats. To add to their difficulty, the river water was murky, so obstacles like sunken trees and rocks were hidden. The pirogues and canoes were always bumping into things and upsetting or taking on water when the men encountered rapids.

At night, everyone slept in Indian-style tents called tepees. These were made of dried buffalo skins tied around a framework of ten or twelve wooden poles. As a mark of their status,

When the corps stopped to camp, they slept in tepees, similar to the ones pictured in this early 20th-century photograph.

Sacagawea, Charbonneau, Baptiste, and the other interpreter, Drouillard, shared the best tent with Lewis and Clark.

Preparing Food

The daily labor was backbreaking and the men were always hungry. From the beginning of the expedition, Sacagawea distinguished herself as a talented, hardworking food gatherer—a skill that was expected of Native American women but which the corps members lacked. Using a sharp stick, she would dig wild artichokes from underground holes where mice had gathered the plant and hoarded it in piles for the winter. The wild artichoke was also called the artichoke thistle, and the stalks were very tasty when peeled and boiled. She also found a sweet plant called wild licorice and a root the corps called the "white apple," a nutritious, starchy tuber that was a staple among many Native American

The wild artichoke pictured here is similar to the variety that Sacagawea picked and prepared for the corps members.

tribes. The corps added this root to soups and gravies to thicken up the often watery mixtures.

In addition to Sacagawea's substantial food contributions, the corps shot and ate a lot of beaver. Their favorite parts were the liver and the fatty tail. They didn't know it then, but their bodies were probably craving the iron and vitamins in the rich organ meat and fat, after their winter of lean deer and elk meat and hard biscuits. Charbonneau would often prepare and cook a sausage that Lewis described in detail in his journal. The interpreter would mix meat, liver, kidney, **suet**, salt, pepper, and flour. He would squeeze out the contents of a buffalo intestine (Lewis wrote that he often did not get *all* of the contents out), and stuff the intestine with the meat mixture. Then, he would tie it off, rinse the sausage in the river, boil it in a copper kettle, and fry it in bear oil until it was done.

Beavers, like the one pictured here, were hunted by the men and used as food. The tail was a particular favorite among members of the corps.

Boating Mishaps

Charbonneau was definitely better at cooking than at sailing. The captains discovered this first on April 13, only five days into the expedition. Charbonneau was manning the tiller of one of the pirogues, which was loaded with mapping instruments, papers, medicine, and trade goods. Sacagawea, Baptiste, and three men, including George Drouillard, were riding in the pirogue. None of the men could swim. Suddenly, a small, sudden storm blew up on the river, knocking the boat over onto its side.

The situation could have been easily remedied but Charbonneau panicked and turned the vessel toward the wind—a bad sailing decision. The pirogue threatened to capsize. Lewis shouted to Drouillard to take over. Drouillard wrestled with the tiller and sails, and after a few tense moments, managed to right and steady the boat. Luckily, there was no loss of equipment—not this time.

Her husband may have panicked under pressure, but soon, during the journey's first major crisis, Sacagawea showed the captains that *she* could remain calm even in a critical situation. On May 14, the corps was paddling as usual. Charbonneau was at the **helm** of one of the pirogues that carried important gear and other corps members, including his wife and son.

. . . Sacagawea showed the captains that she *could remain calm even in a critical situation.*

In a departure from their usual arrangement, both Lewis and Clark happened to be walking on shore. Again, as in April, a dangerous squall slammed into the boats. Once again, Charbonneau panicked and steered the boat straight into the wind. The pirogue turned on its side, sails flapping, and began filling with water. In another moment, the entire boat would capsize, dumping all of its cargo, human and otherwise, into the freezing, rushing Missouri River. Charbonneau, who could not swim, went stiff with fear, and released the tiller entirely. He gripped the sides of the boat and began yelling prayers, begging for divine intervention.

Bang! Bang! Onshore, Lewis and Clark each fired their guns in the air to get the men's attention. They began shouting orders, directing the men to haul in the sails, which were holding the boat pinned on its side. But in the confusion, no one heard them. The situation was dire: This particular pirogue was carrying the papers, instruments, books, medicine, and trade goods—almost all of the group's essential items—and it looked like it was about to capsize completely.

Lewis threw his gun to the ground and began unfastening his coat, preparing to jump in the water and swim to the boat. Luckily, he thought better of it—the river was choppy and he probably never would have made it. For an agonizing thirty seconds, the boat lay on its side, filling with water.

In another moment, the entire boat would capsize, dumping all of its cargo . . . into the freezing, rushing Missouri River.

At last, Pierre Cruzatte, the half-blind fiddler who was seated in the bow of the pirogue, shouted at Charbonneau that he would shoot him immediately if he did not take the tiller to right the boat. Charbonneau somehow gathered himself enough to obey, and Cruzatte, now in charge of the situation, ordered the other two men on board to start rowing to shore. With the boat riding almost totally under the water, the men reached shore and began bailing out the water.

Throughout all of this confusion, Sacagawea sat in the stern of the pirogue, calm and composed. With Baptiste in one arm, she

Many of the supplies carried by the Corps of Discovery were probably held in barrels like the ones shown in this exhibit at Harpers Ferry National Historical Park in West Virginia.

leaned over the edge of the boat and carefully fished out articles that had come loose and were floating by in the water. In the end, she saved so many items that the only things lost were some medical supplies, some gunpowder, and some garden seeds. Of the passengers in the boat, Sacagawea was the only one who thought to rescue the floating items. Lewis later credited her in his journal, saying, "the Indian woman to whom I ascribe equal fortitude and resolution, with any person onboard at the time of the accident, caught and preserved most of the light articles which were washed overboard."

With the pirogue safely ashore and the wet articles unloaded, Lewis and Clark ordered all the men to have a drink of whiskey to help them recover. Each captain took a drink themselves to calm their nerves. A few days later, the captains named a branch of a river for the brave teenager and Lewis recorded in his journal, "this stream we called Sah-ca-ger we-ah or bird woman's River, after our interpreter the Snake woman." Sacagawea was rapidly proving herself to be an indispensable member of the corps.

CHAPTER 7

Near Death and Danger

[The] Indian woman complaining all night & excessively bad this morning. Her case is some what dangerous.

—William Clark

The rest of May proceeded without other tragedies—other than the night that a tree near the captains' tent caught fire, possibly after being struck by lightning. Lewis and Clark and the interpreters, including Sacagawea, just managed to move the tepee moments before the burning tree crashed to the ground right on the spot where the tent had been.

On the days when it was Clark's turn to walk on shore, Sacagawea and Baptiste accompanied him. It was during these long days that Sacagawea and Clark formed what many historians believe was a close **platonic** relationship that would continue throughout the journey. Clark nicknamed Sacagawea "Janey," and she gave him lovely gifts, such as an ermine shoulder covering, on occasion. Clark also became very attached to little Baptiste, whom he called "Pomp."

In early June, after fighting the upstream current for two long months, the corps came to a fork in the river. The mighty Missouri was split, with one branch flowing to the north and the other to the south. After briefly exploring each branch, the captains decided that the south fork was the main river that would

Clark also became very attached to little Baptiste, whom he called "Pomp."

Lewis and Clark stand near the fork of the Marias and Missouri rivers. They decided to take the southern fork, which turned out to be the continuation of the Missouri River.

eventually lead to the Rocky Mountains—and beyond them, the Columbia River. The north fork, they felt, ran too far north, and the south fork was larger with stronger currents. The captains named the north fork—a tributary of the Missouri River—the Marias River. Having made the decision to take the south fork, the group decided to push on. Time was growing short—the summer would be brief out here on the high plains, and they had to cross the Rockies before winter.

Sacagawea Falls Ill

But before they could leave the mouth of the Marias, Sacagawea fell gravely ill. Sickness was common on the journey—every few days, Clark or Lewis would record in their journals that one or another of the men was ill. But Sacagawea's illness seems to have been particularly serious. Her exact symptoms are unknown, but historians have offered a range of opinions on her sickness. From the journals, we know that she had pain in her lower abdomen and groin, and a fever. Sacagawea may have had a pelvic infection or inflammation, or she may have been having a **miscarriage**.

Whatever the specific illness, the captains were very concerned about her. Every day in their journals, they reported on her health status and treatment. Charbonneau may have been concerned also—we don't really know just how he felt about his wife. But as sick as she was, presumably Sacagawea still had to care for Baptiste. He was still nursing and if she died, he might also.

A c. 1804 print shows the medical procedure of bleeding, which Clark performed on Sacagawea when she was very ill.

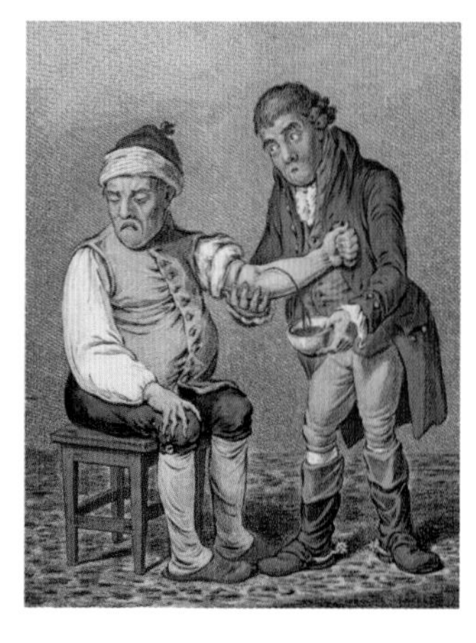

In an effort to help Sacagawea, Clark repeatedly performed a procedure on her called bleeding. It involved opening a patient's vein and allowing the blood to flow out for a time. This was a very common medical treatment for many centuries and was thought to help or cure any number of sicknesses. Now, of course, doctors know that bleeding was not at all helpful. Sick people need all of their blood and the treatment did nothing at best, and, at worst, actively harmed patients.

Not surprisingly, Clark's treatment did not help Sacagawea. She grew worse—so sick that Clark wrote in his journal that he feared she might die. But the expedition could not come to a complete halt. Lewis soon left to explore the Great Falls of the Missouri, as the corps had previously planned. Clark remained with the corps and the sick woman and continued their journey along the south fork.

At night, Sacagawea could lie in her tent, but during the day she had to ride in the pirogue along with everyone else. It must have been miserable for her—sick, trying to nurse and care for the baby Baptiste, all while lying in the hard, rocking canoe under the glaring sun. At last, Clark thought to move her into the shaded part of the pirogue, which probably helped her more than all his bloodletting.

Sacagawea was in terrible pain. The normally stoic and calm girl moaned all of one night. Clark wrote on June 14 that her sickness was now dangerous. Scouring his medicine stores, he dosed her with quinine, a fever-reducer and painkiller that is still occasionally used today to treat malaria. Clark also made Sacagawea a **poultice** of bark, which he applied to her lower abdomen and groin. He probably thought that the heat of the poultice would soothe the pain in those areas. But the sick teenager was not getting better. By June 16, she had become delirious from fever and refused any medication. In desperation, Clark appealed to Charbonneau, saying he must convince his wife to take her medicine.

She grew worse—so sick that Clark wrote in his journal that he feared she might die.

Somehow, Charbonneau managed to get Sacagawea to take the medicine. However, historians have long puzzled over a cryptic entry in Clark's journal during Sacagawea's illness. At one point, he writes, "if She dies it will be the fault of her husband as I am now convinced." Why, historians ask, would Charbonneau be blamed for his wife's death? Some historians speculate that Clark miswrote, intending to say that if she dies, it will *not* be the fault of her husband. Others believe that if Sacagawea was indeed suffering a miscarriage, her death would be his fault, in some sense.

Recovery at Last

Later that same day, Lewis returned from his Great Falls exploration. He found Sacagawea with a weak pulse and a disturbing twitch in her arms and fingers. The twitching probably resulted from a mineral deficiency, mostly likely caused by Clark's bloodletting treatment. He was very concerned, Lewis wrote later in his journal, because they were counting on Sacagawea to help them get horses from the Shoshone.

Drawing on the medicines he had, Lewis did his best to nurse Sacagawea back to health. He dosed her with laudanum, a

Clark treated Sacagawea with doses of laudanum, a painkiller and sedative used during the 19th century. The label on this bottle indicates that using too much could be poisonous.

sedative, to calm her, and applied bark poultices. But probably his most effective treatment was having Sacagawea drink water from a nearby mineral spring. It is believed that this water restored the lost minerals in her blood and calmed her twitching. At last, Sacagawea seemed to be recovering after more than a week of being seriously ill. She began walking around a little each day and fishing in the river.

Relieved, the captains decided to rest near the Great Falls of Missouri. Sacagawea could recuperate there, and they could use the time to prepare the equipment for the **portage** around the Great Falls. Lewis watched Sacagawea's recovery carefully, and allowed her to eat only salted, peppered, broiled buffalo meat and buffalo broth. But Sacagawea was hungry after her illness, and on June 19, she ate a large portion of the "white apple" roots and dried fish. The food was too much for her, and her fever returned. Lewis was furious with Charbonneau, whom he blamed for allowing his wife to stray from her prescribed diet. The next day, though, Sacagawea was better, and by June 24, Lewis wrote, she had recovered.

The crew began the long, arduous portage around the Great Falls, hauling several tons of equipment and boats overland without horses, mules, or oxen to bear some of the load. The

This modern painting depicts corps members portaging tons of equipment around the Great Falls.

The Great Falls

Lewis was probably both thrilled and intimidated when he and his party came upon the Great Falls of the Missouri on June 13, 1805. At the time, the falls measured ninety-six feet high and were made up of five smaller waterfalls, all completely unnavigable by boat, as Lewis must have soon realized. (When the Great Falls were dammed in the early twentieth century, one of the smaller falls was hidden.) Nevertheless, Lewis wrote in his journal that the falls were "the grandest sight I ever beheld. . . . [F]rom the reflection of the sun on the [spray] or mist which [arises] from these falls is a beautiful rainbow produced which adds not a little to the beauty of this majestically grand [scenery]."

Today, the Great Falls are heavily dammed, so little remains of the crashing white water and spray that Lewis admired. A major city, Great Falls, Montana, has grown up near the dams. Visitors to Great Falls can visit the Lewis and Clark National Historic Trail Interpretive Center, but they will have to use their imaginations to envision the landscape that Lewis and Clark saw.

Lewis discovered the spectacular Great Falls, located in present-day Montana.

men built some wooden wagons to help them drag the canoes, but the heavier boats had to be left behind. During the portage, which would take over a month, the captains explored the area. Sacagawea and Baptiste kept their usual routine of walking with Clark during the day.

Storm!

On June 29, Sacagawea, Baptiste, and Charbonneau were walking with Clark as he continued his mapping of the region. Sacagawea carried Baptiste in his cradleboard along with a bundle of baby clothes and bedding. As they walked along the river bank, the wind began to whistle, and Clark pointed out thunderclouds building on the horizon. A storm was coming. They must seek shelter, he told the group. Clark directed everyone to scramble down into a dry gully nearby and huddle underneath some overhanging rocks.

Clutching at bushes and roots, the group lowered themselves down the gully and crouched together, listening for the storm. A massive crack of thunder rolled through the ravine. Rain began to fall, slowly at first, and then increased to a torrent of water mixed with hail. Before anyone realized it, the gully started to fill with water. The hiding place was not safe, but before the group could move, there came a rumbling noise.

Everyone looked up and stared in horror as a massive wave of muddy water came thundering toward them down the ravine, "[tearing] up everything before it" and carrying giant boulders along with it. As the water rose around their waists, Clark moved fast. He shoved Charbonneau, who was frozen with fear, up the side of

Rain began to fall, slowly at first, and then increased to a torrent of water mixed with hail.

the gully with adrenaline-fueled strength. Clark then scrambled up the gully himself, holding his gun in one hand and shoving Sacagawea and Baptiste in front of him. Once Charbonneau reached the top, he reached down and pulled his wife the rest of the way up the high bank.

Safe at last, the group looked down at the gully, now filled with raging brown water. Only a quarter of a mile away, the main river dropped into an eighty-seven foot waterfall. If they had slipped, the gully water would have carried them straight to the river and over the waterfall's edge.

In the onslaught of the storm, Sacagawea had lost Baptiste's cradleboard and all his clothes and bedding, but the baby himself was fine. Clark lost his compass. Everyone was wet and Clark was concerned about Sacagawea—he didn't want her illness to return. He gave her a little sip of whiskey to help her keep warm and everyone began the trek back to the camp, relieved, no doubt, to have survived yet another close call.

When Sacagawea and members of the corps encountered a violent storm, they got caught in a dangerous flash flood—such as the one depicted in this undated painting by Robert Gallon.

CHAPTER 8

In Shoshone Country

I cannot discover that she [shows] any . . . joy in being again restored to her native country. . . . I believe she would be perfectly content anywhere.

—*Meriwether Lewis*

July was a hard month for the corps. It was hot, and every day the crew had to portage gear around the Great Falls. To make matters worse, local tribes told them that the buffalo population had disappeared a little further on. Because buffalo was a source of rich, abundant food for the men, the herd's absence meant lean times ahead.

Once the crew completed the portage around the mighty falls, they found a westward waterway. Around July 15, 1805, they launched their canoes and all their gear to continue their water journey. Excitement rose—they were nearing the land of the Shoshone. Each day, they were seeing signs of the tribe in the area—probably campfire ashes, animal remains, and occasional personal items like discarded moccasins or pots.

One day, on a land walk with Lewis, Sacagawea indicated to him that she recognized the area they were traveling in—it was near the place of her kidnapping.

Excitement rose—they were nearing the land of the Shoshone.

On July 25, Captain Clark, with a small advance party, reached the area known as Three Forks, where three major rivers converged. A few days later, the rest of the corps arrived. This spot, Sacagawea told the men, was the buffalo hunting ground of the Shoshone. Each fall, when the animals were fattest from the summer grass, her tribe would pack their tepees and horses and make the long journey down from their mountain home to the camp, where they would spend the fall hunting, butchering, and drying buffalo meat. Eventually, they would return back to the mountains, carrying with them enough meat to sustain the tribe through the winter.

Sacagawea pointed to a huge limestone outcropping, which towered over the barren landscape. That was Beaverhead Rock, she said through the interpretation string, so called because it resembled the head of a beaver swimming, and it was there that she had crossed the river in a desperate and futile attempt to escape the Hidatsa raiders. She told the story in her usual stoic manner, Lewis wrote later. "I cannot discover that she [shows] any [emotion] of sorrow in recollecting this event, or joy in being again restored to her native country. . . . [I]f she has enough to eat and a few trinkets to wear I believe she would be perfectly content anywhere," he noted. Of course, Sacagawea may have just been keeping her true feelings to herself.

Sacagawea recognized Beaverhead Rock—an indication that the expedition was nearing Shoshone country. One can imagine the head of a beaver when viewing this rock formation in Montana.

Hunting Buffalo

The buffalo, or American bison, was an essential animal to the survival of the Plains Indians. They depended on this huge creature to supply many of their daily needs: meat for food; skins for clothing and tepees; bones for tools, needles, and bowls; and sinew for string and thread. But hunting the buffalo was not an easy task, especially in the days before guns. Buffalo can weigh up to two thousand pounds when fully grown, but they can easily outrun a horse over time and are capable of nimble turns and evasions.

The Shoshone and other Plains Indians developed sophisticated hunting techniques to bring down these huge animals. Sometimes they would build a large pen and drive the animals into the pen, where they were slaughtered. If a cliff was handy, mounted hunters could chase the buffalo over the cliff and then retrieve the carcasses from below. Sometimes hunters would creep up on quietly grazing herds and attempt to shoot an animal. Other times, horsemen would surround and charge a portion of a herd. When the animals began running, the hunters would race up beside them on horseback and shoot them from point-blank range. Eventually, overhunting of the buffalo led to their near-extinction.

A c. 1907 print depicts an Indian buffalo hunt in 1867.

Searching for the Shoshone

The corps members knew they were close to Shoshone country, and they thought they would find the Shoshone off in the hills, not by the river. But there was far too much gear to transport overland without horses. So, on August 9, the captains decided to separate. Lewis and a crew, including the interpreter Drouillard, proceeded westward by land, while Sacagawea, Charbonneau, Clark, and the others traveled with the boats on the river.

Drouillard did not speak Shoshone, but he did know some Indian sign language that Lewis hoped would be enough to communicate with any Indians they met. Why Lewis did not take Sacagawea, the only Shoshone speaker in the corps, is a mystery. Perhaps he believed the overland trek would be too arduous for Baptiste and his mother. Or that her interpreting skills wouldn't be needed until it came time to negotiate for the essential horses. For now, they just needed to find some Shoshone who could take them to the main Shoshone camp.

Almost immediately upon separating from Clark's party, Lewis and the crew found hoofprints on an old road—a sure sign there were horses nearby! The road led them farther upstream along the river, where the water divided into two equal branches. Unsure as to which branch was the main river, Lewis wrote a note to Clark, telling him to stay with the corps at the fork division until Lewis's party came back to get them. He then fastened the note to a pole in the middle of the river.

Why Lewis did not take Sacagawea, the only Shoshone speaker in the corps, is a mystery.

Lewis and the crew proceeded overland. On the second day they encountered a Native American on horseback whom he suspected was Shoshone. Unfortunately, through some verbal miscommunication, the Indian rider became frightened, wheeled on his horse, and galloped away.

Lewis was disappointed but not disheartened. This attempt at communication had failed but they were certainly in Shoshone country. Soon, they would be able to find the tribe—and get the horses.

Undaunted, Lewis's crew continued on. They were heading into the Rocky Mountains. The crew came upon an old Shoshone trail called Lemhi Pass, and on August 12, struggled up the side of a tall mountain, their excitement climbing along with their footsteps. At the top of this hill was the Continental Divide—the line which divides the rivers of the continent into those that flow into the Pacific Ocean and those that flow into the Atlantic Ocean. As he mounted the hill, Lewis turned eager eyes westward. There spreading before him, he hoped, would be the fabled Northwest Passage—the river that would take them to the ocean! But there was no Northwest Passage spread before Lewis's eyes. All he saw were mountain ranges bigger than any he had ever seen, thrusting their craggy gray slopes far into the sky and stretching far to the horizon. The Rockies were far greater than

Lemhi Pass as seen today seems almost untouched. It was here that Lewis and Clark reached the Continental Divide and saw miles of mountain ranges before them.

he—or anyone else—could have ever imagined, and the corps would have to cross them to reach the ocean.

The vastness of the mountains made getting horses all the more imperative—Lewis could see that. There was no earthly way they could transport all of their gear overland without pack animals. They had to make contact with the Shoshone before anything else could happen. Sacagawea would be key to the negotiations.

Making Contact

The next morning, Lewis got his chance. The party crossed down into a ravine and stumbled upon two Shoshone women and a little girl, gathering food. Terrified, one woman ran away, but the other two were frozen in place with fear. They crouched on the ground, heads down, and waited to be killed. Lewis took a little pot of red paint from his pocket. Sacagawea had told him that when he met some Shoshone, Lewis should paint the Shoshone's cheeks with red to show he came in peace. Carefully, Lewis bent and gently rubbed red stripes on the golden cheeks of the woman and little girl. They looked up, and he and Drouillard motioned to them that he wished to be taken to their camp.

Trusting Lewis's kind demeanor and signals of friendship, the woman agreed. She led them out of the ravine. Lewis and his men must have been trying to contain their jubilation—they were on their way to the Shoshone camp. Now maybe they could make some progress.

But as they drew nearer, galloping hooves sounded in the distance and about sixty Shoshone warriors, led by their chief, approached. They were all riding beautiful horses very fast. His heart in his throat, Lewis faced the group head-on, dropping his gun to the ground and holding only a U.S. flag in his hands as a sign of peace.

CHAPTER 9

A Homecoming

[Clark] saw [Sacagawea] . . . [begin] to dance and show every mark of the most extravagant joy . . . sucking her fingers at the same time to indicate they were of her native tribe.

—Nicholas Biddle

Lewis's caution was unnecessary, as it turned out. The Shoshone were overjoyed to see the white men. Everyone dismounted and greeted the visitors in their customary way—with enthusiastic bear hugs. Soon, Lewis and his crew were smeared with paint and oil from the embraces of many warriors, until "I was heartily tired of the national hug," Lewis wrote later. Soon, he hoped, he would be able to find out more about the mountains and the possibility of trading for horses.

The chief, who communicated that his name was Cameahwait, seated everyone—his warriors, Lewis, and his crew—in a circle, on the ground. The chief wanted to determine if Lewis and his men were peaceful and trustworthy. Cameahwait watched as Lewis, like his host, solemnly removed his moccasins. This was an important Shoshone diplomatic gesture. It meant that if a person was not faithful to the promises he made during a **council**, he would swear to go barefoot for the rest of his life. Possibly with Drouillard providing some sign language communication, a pipe was passed and everyone smoked it as a further symbol of peace.

Smoking the pipe of a Native American was a sign of peace. This Shoshone chief named Washakie proudly holds his peace pipe—perhaps in the same manner Cameahwait did when he met with Lewis.

After this first introductory council, Cameahwait apparently felt that he could trust Lewis and his crew enough to lead them to the main Shoshone camp a short distance away. There, the Shoshone conducted a second, more formal council, which took place in a lodge, a very large tent made of tanned buffalo hide. Everyone sat in a circle again, this time on branches and antelope skins, around a large fire. They removed their moccasins once more and Cameahwait again passed around a peace pipe, this time made of polished transparent green stone.

Through signs and with Drouillard's help, Lewis managed to communicate that he and his men were seeking an easy passage through the mountains and on to the Pacific Ocean, possibly via the Salmon River. Cameahwait shook his head emphatically. Drawing a map in the dirt that showed little piles of earth and sticks to represent the mountains and rivers, the chief indicated it was impossible to follow the Salmon to the Pacific, either by boat or by walking its banks. It was far too rough, with rapids and mountains obstructing passage almost the entire way. The Shoshone themselves wouldn't even attempt that route.

The chief wanted to determine if Lewis and his men were peaceful and trustworthy.

But, the Shoshone told him, there *was* a mountain pass to the north and west, though it would mean packing everything overland. Lewis noted that the Shoshone appeared to have many beautiful horses—animals that were obviously of high value. Careful negotiation and hard trading would be required to obtain enough for the trip. Would Sacagawea be able to strike a bargain deal?

Holding Council

Through Drouillard's signs, Lewis indicated to Cameahwait that the chief and his men should go with Lewis so that they could meet Clark and his canoes full of provisions and trade goods.

But Cameahwait was suspicious. What if this was some sort of trap? What if these white men were in league with the enemy Blackfeet tribe? He and his warriors could be walking straight into an enemy ambush. Finally though, with Lewis and Drouillard's combined efforts, the chief reluctantly agreed, and the group set out for the river fork, where Clark, Sacagawea, Charbonneau, and the other crewmen would be waiting.

Surely, Lewis thought, once they reached the meeting place and Cameahwait saw Clark and Sacagawea, he would realize they were telling the truth. But, "when we arrived in sight at the distance of about 2 miles I discovered to my mortification that the party had not yet arrived."

His heart sank. Clark, Sacagawea, and the rest of the corps had not yet reached the

Although Sacagawea was not with them, Drouillard, shown in this modern painting, did a credible job of communicating with Cameahwait.

meeting place. Lewis nervously watched as suspicion gathered on Cameahwait's face once more. If the Shoshone left, the chance of horses left with them, along with the hope of crossing the Rockies.

Lewis drew on his resolve. He unholstered his gun and handed it solemnly to Cameahwait. He gestured to his men to do the same, and one by one, each pulled out his own weapon and handed it over to the Shoshone. This was a powerful gesture. Lewis was saying, in effect, that he was ceding control of the situation to the Shoshone, and that they need not fear a trap.

All day, the group played a waiting game. Lewis wrote in his journal of the tension he felt—hoping that the Shoshone would trust them and not kill them. The air in the camp was tense enough to cut with a knife. Everyone was watching one another. Were the Shoshone just waiting for an ambush? Were Lewis and his men to be shot any moment? But Lewis, displaying remarkable strength, refused to show how concerned he was. He made sure he appeared only relaxed and cheerful to the Indians, so that they would not see just how worried he was. Each hour that passed without Clark's party only added to the tension around camp.

If the Shoshone left, the chance of horses left with them, along with the hope of crossing the Rockies.

Lewis tried to reassure the chief by telling him of Sacagawea. "I mentioned to the chief several times that we had with us a woman of his nation . . . and that by means of her I hoped to explain myself more fully than I could do signs." Sacagawea's language skills would be essential for the protracted and nuanced trading ahead of them.

Finally, the next morning, a Shoshone scout raced back into camp, shouting that he had seen white men dragging boats up the river. Immediately, the tension in the camp evaporated. All suspicion was forgiven, and the Shoshone and white men alike ran around hugging each other with joy.

A Joyful Reunion

Everyone watched as the figures on the river drew closer. Most of the men were rowing the boats, but Clark, Sacagawea, and Charbonneau were walking onshore in their usual fashion. As the party on foot drew close enough to see who was ahead of them, Sacagawea, ordinarily so restrained, threw off her usual calm demeanor and began to dance joyfully while sucking on her fingers—a sign that indicated these people were the ones who had nurtured her. Lewis had not only found the Lemhi Shoshone, he had found Sacagawea's own band, whom she had not seen in six or seven years.

All of the Shoshone rushed out to meet them as they approached. As they came nearer to the camp, Sacagawea recognized someone in the crowd—Jumping Fish, the girl who had been kidnapped with her and had escaped. Corps member Nicholas Biddle later wrote that the two girls "embraced with the most tender affection. The meeting of the two young women had in it something peculiarly touching, not only in the ardent manner in which their feelings were expressed, but from the real interest of their situation." Even the usually emotionless Lewis noted that the reunion between the two was quite touching.

. . . Sacagawea, ordinarily so restrained, threw off her usual calm demeanor and began to dance joyfully. . . .

While Sacagawea and Jumping Fish were having their reunion, Cameahwait invited the captains into his tent, along with some other Shoshone. Clark, in recognition of his status as captain and new guest, was seated on a white robe and had six white shells tied in his red hair. Everyone took off their moccasins, passed the peace pipe, and prepared to talk—finally.

Sacagawea quietly entered the tent and sat down, prepared to interpret. She began to translate when she looked up at the group for the first time. To the amazement of everyone in the lodge, Sacagawea cried out, leapt from her robe, threw a blanket over herself and Cameahwait, and hugged him in a flood of tears. Weeping, she told Lewis and Clark that Cameahwait was not just any Shoshone, but her very own brother! The coincidence was extraordinary, the captains wrote in their journals, and Cameahwait was also moved by seeing his sister again, though, the captains noted, not as much as Sacagawea.

After being reunited with her brother, Cameahwait, Sacagawea proudly introduces him to her baby, Jean-Baptiste.

Tough Negotiations

Sacagawea sat back down and tried to resume interpreting, though she kept having bouts of joyful tears. The translation chain moved forward slowly, with Sacagawea translating from Shoshone to Hidatsa for Charbonneau, Charbonneau speaking in French to Labiche, and Labiche translating to English for the captains. Sacagawea told Cameahwait that Lewis and Clark wanted to trade

Packhorses, such as the ones shown in this c. 1908 photograph with a Native American woman, were essential for the expedition's mountain crossing.

for packhorses to help their mountain crossing, and that they wanted Shoshone guides to take them through the northern passage. In turn, Cameahwait informed the captains that above all, he wanted to trade for guns so that the Shoshone could better defend themselves against the well-armed Blackfeet. With guns, Cameahwait said, the tribe could come down from the mountains more often to hunt in the fertile valleys, where there was more game and less snow. With the trade requests laid out, but not yet agreed upon, the council concluded.

Following the council, Sacagawea learned either from Cameahwait or a fellow Shoshone that the rest of her family was dead: her mother, father, and her sister. There is no record of her reaction to this news, but judging from her joy at seeing her brother, she must have been heartbroken. Then, a little boy was brought out and presented to Sacagawea. He was the son of her dead sister, her own nephew, someone told her. With her typical generosity, Sacagawea adopted him immediately, though he had to remain with the tribe, of course. She also made a present of a precious lump of white sugar to Cameahwait, who had never tasted it before. He told her that it was the best food he had ever eaten.

But not all of the family reunion was joyful. The other person Sacagawea met during that whirlwind day was the man to whom she had been promised so many years before. He was more than twice her age and already had two wives. He told Sacagawea that he did not want her as a wife now, because she already had a child by another man. We do not know if Sacagawea was affected by this. Perhaps she didn't care. Or perhaps his unkind words left a pang.

A Whirl of Activity

There was no time to waste. Though it was only late August, they could still expect snow up in the mountains, and the corps had no idea how long the crossing would take. While Lewis and a crew hauled equipment and gear from the river to the camp, Clark and others, including Sacagawea and Cameahwait, went to explore the Salmon River route the Shoshone had recommended against. The captains just weren't quite ready to give up on the hope that they might be able to travel by canoe through the Rockies.

The other person Sacagawea met during that whirlwind day was the man to whom she had been promised so many years before.

Clark might have saved himself the effort. He found exactly what the Shoshone had said he would: a completely impassable river, full of rapids, and with banks so rugged that horses could barely traverse them, even without loads of gear. They would have to take the northwestern mountain pass, Clark reported back at the camp, and travel over land, at least through the mountains. Perhaps on the other side they would be able to pick up the Columbia River, which would take them through to the Pacific.

Lewis and Clark appealed to Cameahwait for his final decision and the chief agreed: He would trade twenty-nine horses in exchange for pistols, gunpowder, and knives. It was settled—the journey could proceed! Cameahwait promised to bring the horses from the main Shoshone camp.

The men got busy preparing for the trip. At a spot they called Camp Fortunate, near the Jefferson River, they dug underground **caches** secretly, out of sight of the Shoshone, and hid gear they wouldn't need for the rest of the trip. They also filled the canoes and pirogues with stones and sunk them in the river, where they would remain until they came back. In addition to keeping the wood of the boats moist, the sunken boats would be safe from animals and thieves.

Plans for the next phase of the expedition were now underway and, most importantly, the horses and guides were assured . . . or so the corps thought.

A Failed Plot

By August 23, Lewis was getting nervous. The corps would need to start the crossing right away, he told Cameahwait. They must reach the Pacific by snowfall. But the chief told him that he wanted to wait for another group of Shoshone guides to arrive. Lewis reluctantly agreed to wait. When the Shoshone group finally caught up to the corps, they told Lewis and Clark they were all going down into the valley for the annual buffalo hunt. A warning bell went off in Lewis's head. It was true that the time for the hunt was drawing near. Was it possible that Cameahwait and his men would abandon them and go on the hunt? With such a delay, the expedition would fail. They *had to* have the horses and guides now if they were to cross the mountains before winter.

The next day, the corps and its Shoshone guides, including the chief, finally set out for the West. Most walked, but Sacagawea rode a horse that Charbonneau had bought for her. Along the way, Sacagawea learned that the captains' early suspicions were correct. Someone had told her that Cameahwait was planning to leave the corps and take his men to the buffalo hunt, without giving Lewis and Clark the horses or guides he had promised. Sacagawea told Charbonneau what she had learned and Charbonneau, presumably through Labiche, told Lewis and Clark. The captains confronted the chief, who admitted that the news was true. His people were hungry, he told them, and needed to hunt. Nonetheless, he was a man of his word, he said, and sent a messenger to the rest of the tribe, retracting his order to gather for the hunt. He would stay with the corps and trade them the horses.

Was it possible that Cameahwait and his men would abandon them and go on the hunt?

The expedition was saved, for the time being, by Sacagawea. If she had kept the rumor to herself, Lewis and Clark might well have been stranded in the mountains—their only option to turn back east. But she chose to tell the captains of her brother's treacherous plans. Sacagawea never gave an explanation for this decision, but we can only guess that at this point in the journey, she saw herself as a member of the corps—and for now, her future was with them.

CHAPTER 10

Crossing the Rocky Mountains

[As] Soon as they Saw [Sacagawea] . . . they pointed to her. . . . [T]he sight of This Indian woman . . . confirmed our friendly intentions.

—*William Clark*

As Sacagawea and the Corps of Discovery began their trek into the Rocky Mountains, they climbed endlessly through pine forests and dense underbrush. The horses were all heavily loaded and the men walked beside them, slipping on loose dirt and rocks under their feet. Sacagawea, though, rode her horse, with Baptiste in a cradleboard tied to the saddle. Gradually, the pine trees grew smaller and thinner, and the underbrush disappeared. The rocks became larger, and the slopes steeper. The horses began to struggle under their heavy loads. Their hooves were bruised from the sharp rocks. Sometimes, the men would carry the horses' loads on their own backs, when the animals couldn't otherwise make it.

As Sacagawea and the Corps of Discovery began their trek into the Rocky Mountains, they climbed endlessly through pine forests and dense underbrush.

Along the way, the expedition was aided by the Salish tribe. A camp of Salish tepees in the Rocky Mountains is shown in this c. 1910 image.

After a few days, the captains calculated that they had crossed a mountain at seven thousand feet—the tallest peak of the journey. The weather was rotten: rain, snow, and then sleet. The leather clothing worn by the corps members was frozen and wet. A horse slipped down a hill, throwing its load against a tree and breaking the last thermometer and Clark's writing desk.

On September 4, the members of the corps had a brief rest when they met some members of the friendly Salish tribe. The chief, Three Eagles, and his men were on their way to meet the Shoshone for the hunt. The men refreshed themselves with the Salish's roots and berries, and exchanged some tired horses for fresh ones.

After two days with the Salish, the corps reluctantly left the relative safety of the camp. Time was essential—they must keep traveling in order to make it to the Pacific before winter. Besides, food was extremely scarce and the Salish had barely enough for themselves, much less thirty-three hungry adults.

Throughout the crossing over the Rockies, the journals make no mention of Sacagawea, but she was there. Most likely she rode her horse, or after the animal gave out, walked like everyone else. She probably tried to keep warm and dry and searched for bits of plants to gather. Of course, she was enduring the same hardships and conditions as everyone else, yet she was the only one caring for another human being—Baptiste, who was about six months old at that time.

Dark Days

As the expedition journeyed along the Bitterroot Mountain Range, they encountered a nightmare of constant cold, knee-deep snow, dwindling provisions, and treacherous mountain slopes. Patrick Gass, the carpenter of the corps, wrote later that they traveled over "the most terrible mountains I ever beheld." The views must have been truly stunning, but no one was in the mood to admire nature—they were too busy trying to keep themselves and their animals alive long enough to make it out of the mountains.

Food had become a major concern. They had berries, but they were out of both flour and meat. Only a little corn remained. The crew had to have calories, not only to nourish them, but to help them keep warm. Yet the hunters could not find game. The snow kept sliding off the branches as they passed underneath, so that most days, they walked soaking wet all day. The horses slipped and fell constantly, dumping their packs, which had to be retied and loaded again.

By September 16, two colts had been killed for meat. Morale had never been lower. The corps could not afford to kill more

The Bitterroot Mountains, as seen in this photograph, were a difficult range for the expedition to cross.

horses, and on September 18 there was no supper for anyone. On September 19, they came upon a stray horse, which they immediately caught and ate. More than likely, Sacagawea refused the horse meat. The Shoshone abhorred eating horses and dogs, whom they considered close companions. For her, it would have been akin to **cannibalism**.

What was Sacagawea thinking through those long, snowy days? Perhaps she refused to even think of dying. Or perhaps she bravely accepted the possibility that she and her son might die on this trip.

The men were weak from exposure and hunger. They fell frequently along with their horses. Finally, on September 20, Clark and an advance team of hunters descended out of the Rockies into what is now eastern Idaho. The rest of the crew followed two days later. The arduous journey that had taken them over two weeks would today take three hours by car on a paved road.

Guests of the Nez Perce

As the advance team staggered down out of the mountains, they were greeted by the wonderful sight of green and brown grasses stretching for miles before them. They had reached the Weippe Prairie, a small, grassy plain near present-day Clearwater County, Idaho. In the spring and summer, the Weippe Prairie was a place of extraordinary beauty: rolling grassland covered thickly with the blue flowers of the **camas** plant. This was the land of the vast Nez Perce tribe, which numbered over four thousand.

Once out on the prairie, Clark and his group found three little Nez Perce boys playing in the grass. He gave them ribbons so that they wouldn't run away and they agreed to lead the men to their camp. The Nez Perce welcomed the corps with food and shelter. Over the next few days, the men gorged themselves on the

The beautiful Weippe Prairie was home to the Nez Perce tribe. It was the first sight the corps members saw when they descended from their difficult trek through the mountains.

abundant Nez Perce fare of dried salmon, berries, and camas-root bread. But the crew, half-starved for weeks, could not handle the bread made from this mild root.

The next morning, the men lay strewn over the ground, some on their blankets, some just lying by the fires, all holding their stomachs and groaning. Everyone, including Lewis, suffered from bad diarrhea and stomach cramps. Some could barely ride. Others were so ill, they had to lie on the ground for a spell before mounting their horses.

This was the land of the vast Nez Perce tribe, which numbered over four thousand.

We do not know if Sacagawea was also sick. Presumably she ate the same foods as the men, but perhaps she was wiser and had only a little bit at first. The men themselves slowly recovered over the next few days, especially after they killed a horse for the meat—a diet to which their bodies were more accustomed.

Once recovered, the captains began planning the next step of the journey. None of the interpreters spoke the Nez Perce language, so Drouillard helped them communicate with the tribe using signs, drawings, and gestures. The captains conferred at length with the Nez Perce chief Twisted Hair, who advised them on the best route to the Pacific. They would have to travel down three rivers for twelve days to reach the ocean. He warned them that the rapids they would encounter would be difficult to navigate, but not impossible.

The corps had traveled by horse over the Rockies, but now they were ready to travel by canoe. Using only their hand tools, they felled two massive cottonwood trees and made two canoes that would carry all of the members of the corps. They buried their saddles and branded their horses so that they could reclaim them later, and left the animals with the Nez Perce for safekeeping. In the meantime, the captains busily traded with Twisted Hair for food stores. Though they would be traveling through fertile country once more, Lewis and Clark did not want to endure the slightest risk of hunger after their mountain ordeal.

Statues in Idaho depict the meeting of Lewis and Clark and a Nez Perce Indian.

Making Dugout Canoes

Dugout canoes like the ones the corps made at the Nez Perce camp were a common mode of transportation on the rivers of the United States in the early days of the country. Cottonwood trees, such as Lewis and Clark used, were a good choice since they grew straight, thick, and tall. Their wood was tough and they usually grew near water.

To make a dugout canoe, a traveler would first have to cut down a big tree and trim off all the branches. Using hand tools, he would strip all the bark off the tall trunk, and shape the ends so that they could easily cut through the water. He would then smooth and shape the canoe bottom. To form the interior of the canoe, the builder would gouge out the inner wood of the trunk and make a small, careful fire in the depression. He would let the fire burn some of the wood and then scrape out the burned part, guiding the fire so that it only burned the center of the log. When the burning was done, the canoe-maker would scrape out all the charred wood and smooth the inside so that people could ride in it.

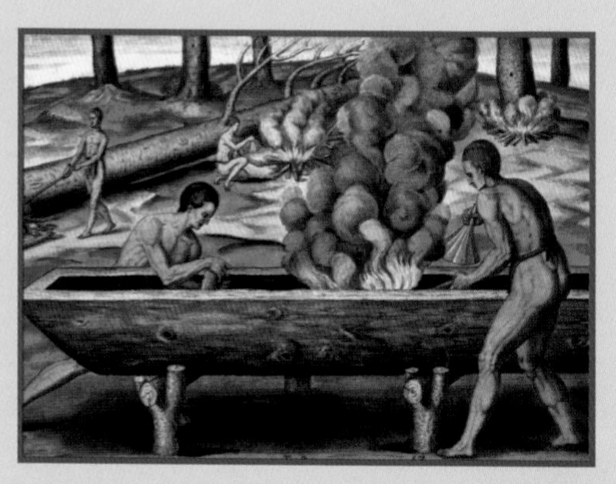

A 1590 engraving shows how ancient natives made dugout canoes by burning the wood, then scraping out the burnt portions to create a depression.

By October 7, the men and Sacagawea were ready to begin canoeing down the waterway known as the Clearwater River.

Riding Down the Rivers

The men of the corps had traded for several Nez Perce guides to help them through the rapids. These men sat in the sterns of the canoes, and, onshore, other Nez Perce walked ahead, explaining their presence to the many other Native Americans who were camped on the shore of the Clearwater. For the first time on the trip, the men experienced the exhilaration of traveling with the fast current of the river, instead of rowing and pulling against the currents of the Missouri.

The only trouble they encountered were the fierce rapids that boiled and foamed in front of their heavy canoes. Moving swiftly through the churning rapids, the bottom of one canoe was damaged by the rocks. Another sank, throwing the men who could not swim into the raging waters. Luckily both the men and the canoe were pulled from the water. Finally, the captains asked the Nez Perce guides to paddle their own canoe in front of the corps's boats so they could show crewmembers the calmest route. This method drastically reduced damage from the rapids.

By October 16, the group reached the Columbia River, which would take them all the way to the Pacific Ocean. Spirits must have been running high. The Native Americans they

A painting by Frederic Remington shows Lewis and Clark, Sacagawea, and other members of the expedition resting along the shore of the Columbia River.

met—mostly of the Yakima and Wanapum tribes—had beads and copper and brass ornaments, items they had gotten from white traders. This was a sure sign they were nearing the Pacific, where trade ships often anchored.

But the Corps of Discovery was not out of danger yet. On October 19, they came upon some Wallawalla Indians, who appeared unfriendly because they thought the expedition was part of a war party. After a few tense moments, however, the Wallawalla spotted Sacagawea, and the tension disappeared. They believed that no war party would ever travel with a woman, so they reasoned that Lewis and Clark must be telling the truth: They were men of peace. Once again, Sacagawea had diffused a threatening situation. Lewis and Clark had always expected Sacagawea to help as an interpreter, but now she was serving yet another function within the corps—that of goodwill ambassador.

This 1905 watercolor by Charles Russell depicts the encounter of the expedition with unfriendly Native Americans along the river. Sacagawea speaks to them as the corps members look on.

CHAPTER 11

A Winter in the Rain

[S]he had traveled a long way with us to See the great waters and that now that monstrous fish was also to be Seen, She thought it verry hard that She Could not be permitted to See either.

—Meriwether Lewis

As they sailed down the Columbia, excitement among the corps members rose. The river was getting wider and fog was settling in the low areas—an indication that they were nearing the sea. The air was soft and moist and it rained almost every day. The expedition was about to reach its goal—and miraculously without one death or serious injury. Though there is no record of her feelings, Sacagawea must have been excited, too. She had traveled so far and had reunited with her people. Now, she would soon see the great water of the Pacific she had heard so much about!

Reaching the Pacific Coastline

By November 7, 1805, the captains judged that they had reached the Pacific coast. However, they were still twenty miles from the ocean. They couldn't paddle all the way to the mouth of the river, and the water was already rocking with waves. Sacagawea reported feeling nauseated, along with some of the other men. Seasickness was a brand-new feeling for those who did not live near open seas with waves.

There was little time for celebration. The weather was terrible and the crew had no shelter. Rain pounded their heads, thunder crashed, and lightning flared overhead. The corps members made a quick camp on the bank of the river and immediately went about trying to get their bearings. Some of the men set off to see if there were any trading vessels at the mouth of the Columbia. The captains began their usual routine of establishing relations with the tribes of the area and explaining their mission.

By November 7, 1805, the captains judged that they had reached the Pacific coast.

The Native Americans who made their homes nearby were the Chinook, Tillamook, and Clatsop. Because of their proximity to the coast, they were used to seeing white men from the trading ships. But the corps members were all worn out from the long trip

One of the Native American groups encountered by the expedition was the Chinook tribe. This c. 1910 print shows a Chinook standing on the riverbank of the Columbia River, where the expedition passed by.

and appeared dirty, unattractive, and unkempt. The impression they presented may not have been ideal, as the captains noted that the Clatsop Indians were the cleanest and friendliest of all of the Native Americans they had met.

Soon, crew members returned from the coast with bad news: There were no trading vessels anchored at the mouth of the Columbia. The corps would have to winter on the coast and travel back overland by spring.

Nonetheless, spirits remained high. They had reached their goal, and even though winter was near, it would be mild here in the temperate Pacific Northwest. On November 24, the captains held a meeting to decide where to set up their winter camp. This meeting was fairly unusual in that each and every member of the corps, including York, Clark's slave, and Sacagawea, was permitted to cast a vote—and each vote was recorded. Ordinarily, the opinions of a slave and a Native American woman would be considered inconsequential. Sacagawea's vote displayed her usual practicality. They had almost starved not too long ago and winter was coming. Therefore, the most important consideration was food. Sacagawea, Clark recorded, voted in favor of a spot with plenty of roots that they could gather to eat through the winter.

The crew eventually chose a high spot, above the coastal marshes and in a protected grove of pine trees. The Clatsop tribe would be their nearest neighbors. Once again, as they had done many months before at Fort Mandan, the men built cabins and a stockade under the direction of Patrick Gass, using only their axes and hand tools. The friendly Clatsop stopped by frequently to watch the progress of the building, often bringing gifts of berries and roots, which the hungry men gratefully accepted. The expedition named the quarters Fort Clatsop.

Upon reaching the coastline of the Pacific, the corps members started building a camp as depicted in this print.

Life on the Coast

The Pacific Coast was treating the corps well, except for one major factor—the weather. Though it wasn't cold or snowy, and no one's ears were freezing off, it rained virtually every single day, all day long. Pacific Coast rain is famous, even today, and the men were bearing the brunt of it. Altogether, the corps would have only twelve days through the entire winter without rain, and only six of those would be sunny. What is more, the temperature was warm, which was certainly not uncomfortable, except that the crew's leather clothes and gear were rotting through, since they could never get the leather completely dry. More importantly, the warm, wet weather made preserving meat almost impossible. Whenever the hunters brought in elk or deer, everyone had to eat as much fresh meat as they could and then put up with spoiled meat after that.

Meanwhile, the captains traded—or attempted to trade—with the Clatsop. But unlike the tribes of the interior, the Clatsop had had years of contact with white traders. Handkerchiefs and medals, the usual goods the captains offered, were of little interest to them. They wanted more practical and valuable items: guns, knives, blankets, and most importantly, blue beads. All across the country, blue beads were valued more highly by Native Americans than beads of any other color. The blue glass beads weren't any different from other beads, except in color, but they may have been more rare, which made them more valuable.

Unfortunately, Lewis and Clark had traded away all of their blue beads and had none left to offer. One Clatsop had an otter skin robe that Lewis coveted deeply. He had never seen otter skin before and admired its sleekness and sheen. For reasons that no one really knows, Sacagawea gave up her own blue beaded belt to Lewis to trade for the robe. In return, the captain gave her a coat of blue wool. No one knows if Sacagawea volunteered her belt once she saw how much Lewis wanted the robe, or if he just took it from her. But judging from the value of her belt, it is not likely that she considered the wool coat an equal replacement.

All the while, the men were working at breakneck speed to finish the fort and get some shelter from the rain. On Christmas Eve, the cabins were complete, and at last everyone could move indoors. Christmas Day of 1805 dawned gray and rainy like all of the rest. But the corps was in a celebratory mood nonetheless. The men woke their captains with a gun salute outside their window. Everyone sang a few carols, probably in French and English, and the captains handed out gifts: tobacco for those who smoked, and silk handkerchiefs for those who didn't. As a sign of their close relationship, Sacagawea gave Clark two dozen white weasel tails. If he gave her a present in return, there is no record of it.

Native American Trade Goods

Trading was an essential part of Native American life—just as essential as buying things in a store would be today. For millennia, Native Americans traded with one another, but when Europeans began spreading across North America, they brought their own trade goods with them. Certain European items became more valuable as trade goods than others: Copper kettles were useful to many tribes. The kettles were lightweight and easily transportable, and when they wore out, they could be cut up to make jewelry and decorations, or even rolled to make copper beads. Knives were another popular item, but in the early days of European–Native American contact, guns were not as popular as you might think. Early guns were big and clumsy, and it was easy to run out of ammunition, leaving the owner with a useless weapon. Later on, as guns spread across the continent and gun technology improved, they became one of the most popular trade goods. Colorful cloth coats were another favorite, as were mirrors, and, of course, glass beads. All of these things, when either worn or carried, showed that the owner was a wealthy person of high status.

Indians traded their precious animal skins for practical items, such as copper pots, knives, and guns. A 1785 drawing depicts such a trade.

Journey to the Whale

Soon after Christmas, Lewis, sick of rotten meat, sent five men to the coastal beaches to set up a primitive **saltworks**, so that the corps could collect salt for preserving meat. While the men were camped on the beach, collecting ocean water and boiling it down, they made friends with some of the Tillamook tribe, who lived nearby. The Tillamook gave them some whale blubber, which the men had never tasted before. They thought it was delicious—like fatty beaver tails, but better. The Tillamook had gotten the blubber from a whale that had washed up on a beach farther away, and there was more to be had. The behemoth was lying right on the sand, waiting for the picking.

The behemoth was lying right on the sand, waiting for the picking.

The men hastened back to the fort and quickly told their captains everything they had heard. Seeing the opportunity for some food other than rotten elk, Clark immediately began organizing a party to travel to the coast and secure some whale meat and blubber. Sacagawea was not included, of course, since she was not a hunter. But something in her must have been building up. She had traveled all this way with these men, had worked just as hard as any of them and endured just as many ordeals. She wanted to see that whale, she told Clark. "[She] had traveled a long way with us to See the great waters and that now that monstrous fish was also to be Seen, She thought it verry hard that She Could not be permitted to See either," Clark wrote in his journal. The captains agreed and allowed her to make the trip.

The journey was arduous. It took five days for Clark's party, including Sacagawea and Baptiste, to reach the coast. They started in canoes but abandoned the vessels after fighting high winds.

Tillamook Head, as shown in this photograph, was a treacherous climb to undertake. Sacagawea attempted it with Jean-Baptiste on her back just so she could see the "monstrous fish."

Then they trudged on foot through a marsh and waded through several creeks. Everyone must have been tired by this time, but the hardest part was yet to come. The party began to climb what is today known as Tillamook Head, about 1,200 feet above sea level. For two hours, the group scrambled up an almost vertical face, pulling themselves up by roots and bushes, eventually ascending one thousand feet. When it came time to descend, they were faced with a slope full of slippery clay, and huge rugged rocks that hung out in midair. Any misstep would cause one to plummet from the cliff into the ocean. Sacagawea somehow made this descent with the added weight of a one-year-old baby on her back.

All safely descended, though, and after a lot more walking and another creek to wade, they finally came to the place where the whale was lying on the beach. The animal, probably a blue whale, had been washed up on a large rock near present-day Cannon Beach, Oregon. Unfortunately, the group had arrived too late. The Tillamook had picked it completely clean. Only the 105-foot skeleton remained.

Eager for Home

Back at the fort, the rain continued unabated. For three months, through January, February, and March, it rained. The men were malnourished and susceptible to disease. Sand fleas, tiny biting insects, were living in everyone's clothes and tormenting the corps constantly. Everyone was ready to leave and tried to hasten the time for their departure by repairing their gear and oiling and repairing the guns.

There was one problem, however. They needed one more canoe, which they didn't have. What's more, they had almost no trade goods left, and the Clatsop wanted a high price for a canoe. So, on March 18, out of desperation, four members of the corps snuck into the Clatsop camp and took a canoe. Lewis told his men that it was okay because the Clatsop had stolen elk meat from them during the winter. Many historians have pointed out that this behavior was very unlike the captains, who generally tried to treat the native tribes in a kind, respectful manner—the same type of behavior that had been shown to them, especially by the Clatsop chief.

Finally, in late March, the gear was ready and the captains had decided that the danger of winter weather was past. The crew loaded the canoes, as they had done so many times before. Lewis and Clark gave Fort Clatsop to the Clatsop chief who had been so kind to them. On March 23, 1806, in the rain as usual, the corps members took their places in the canoes, Sacagawea with Baptiste in his cradleboard and Charbonneau by her side. The Corps of Discovery was going home.

This replica of Fort Clatsop stands at the Lewis and Clark National Historic Park in Oregon.

CHAPTER 12

Eastward Bound

The [I]ndian woman who has been of great Service to me as a pilot through this Country recommends a gap in the mountain more South which I shall cross.

—William Clark

The hunting improved almost immediately as the crew moved away from the coast. Everyone was heartily sick of rotten elk and bought some dogs to eat from the first tribe they could. Sacagawea, of course, would have refused the dog meat, but she would have partaken of the geese, ducks, sturgeon, and roots the corps soon collected. The captains knew it was essential to gather as much meat as possible—there was no guarantee of Native American assistance until they reached their friends the Nez Perce just west of the mountains.

Despite the need to stockpile food, most of the crew's energy was spent trying to guide the canoes against the whitewaters of the Columbia River. The rapids, swollen from spring snow melt, pounded at the rowers day after day, eventually causing one canoe to upset entirely. Unlike the wild ride on the way down the river, the crew struggled against the currents once again. At one point, the captains glumly estimated that the crew had only traveled seven miles in three days of near-constant rowing.

By April 29, the crew had reached the land of the Wallawalla tribe, near the junction of the Snake and Columbia rivers in what is now southern Washington.

Seaman's Disappearance

Lewis and Clark wrote in their journals that the tribes they encountered along the Columbia River on their way home were dirty, diseased, and dishonest. They probably felt that their opinions were confirmed when they woke up one morning to find Seaman the dog missing. He had been stolen in the night by a nearby tribe, the Wah-clel-lar. Lewis was distraught and treated the disappearance as if a human member of the crew had been kidnapped. He immediately organized a rescue party and sent them out with instructions to fight if necessary and bring the dog back alive. The rescuers easily found the dog and his kidnappers, who ran away at the sight of the guns. After that Lewis ordered that any Native American caught fooling with their gear should be instantly shot. He was soothed slightly the next day when a chief came to apologize for the dog thieves and to explain that the behavior was not typical of his tribe.

Lewis was very fond of his dog, Seaman. Today, this 1,400-pound steel sculpture of Lewis's Newfoundland dog can be seen at the Seaman Overlook in Washburn, North Dakota.

The trip along the whitewaters of the Columbia River was treacherous—and this time the corps was going against the current. The rapids caused a canoe to turn over, in a similar way to the canoe shown in this 19th-century engraving.

The captains had met the chief, Yellept, on their outward journey. In their haste to reach the Pacific, they had refused Yellept's invitation to stay and visit. This time, they eagerly accepted the old chief's hospitality and, by a stroke of luck, were able to communicate with him. A Shoshone woman was being held prisoner by the tribe, and through her, Sacagawea was able to interpret during a council. As a symbol of his friendship, Yellept gave Clark a beautiful white horse, and in return, Clark gave the chief a sword.

But the captains needed more horses for the upcoming Rocky Mountain crossing. Earlier, they had been able to exchange two of their cooking kettles for four horses, and Clark had obtained two more when he provided medical care for a tribal chief's wife. The Wallawalla, it turned out, also wanted Clark to provide medicine for some of their illnesses, and were willing to offer horses as payment. These, combined with the horses left with the Nez Perce, would give the corps enough for the mountain crossing.

The Wallawalla . . . also wanted Clark to provide medicine for some of their illnesses, and were willing to offer horses as payment.

In exchange for horses, Clark provided medical help for some of the Indians using medicines he brought along in his medical chest. A similar type of medical kit is shown here.

By May 3, 1806, the group had reached Nez Perce land once more. The captains were pleased to see the horses they had left with the tribe the previous summer were in good condition, as were the saddles and other gear buried in the underground caches. No one was in any hurry to leave the idyllic Weippe Prairie and so the corps wound up staying with the Nez Perce for over a month. The men hunted, butchered, and dried meat for the mountain crossing. Sacagawea gathered a large amount of fennel root, which no one had tasted before and all thought delicious. Every night, Pierre Cruzatte played his fiddle and the corps and Nez Perce danced together around the fires.

Baptiste Falls Ill

For Sacagawea, though, not all of her stay with the Nez Perce was relaxing—most, in fact, was fraught with anxiety. Little Baptiste, who was only a year and three months old, fell seriously ill on May 22. Children frequently died of disease in those days due to lack of modern, effective medications and vaccines, so

Sacagawea must have been very concerned. No one knew what was wrong with Baptiste. He had a sore throat, swollen neck glands, a fever, and a bad case of diarrhea—a serious condition that could kill a child in the course of a few days if not properly treated.

Modern historians have speculated that Baptiste was suffering from **mumps**, tonsillitis, an **abscess** of some sort, or perhaps mastoiditis, a kind of severe ear infection. But of course, there were no drugs to treat any of those conditions. The captains were very concerned about the little boy—especially Clark, who had grown very attached to him during the long days walking on shore with Sacagawea. Clark dosed the boy with a mixture of cream of tartar and sulphur and put a hot poultice of wild onion on his neck. But it did no good—young Baptiste was growing sicker, and the crew became resigned to his death.

. . . young Baptiste was growing sicker, and the crew became resigned to his death.

For five days, Baptiste continued to be very ill, and then on May 27, he appeared to be recovering. Clark kept massaging his neck, this time with a salve of pine resin, beeswax, and bear oil. Lewis also administered some medical treatment that helped to clean out the boy's system. Finally, on June 8, the captains reported that Sacagawea's son was out of danger and almost fully recovered. Every day for eighteen days, each captain had noted Baptiste's condition in their journals.

With the baby's illness behind her, Sacagawea got busy gathering and drying fennel roots for the mountain crossing. The hunters went out for meat every day. No one intended to have a repeat of the last year's crossing. With the horses from the Wallawalla and those left with the Nez Perce over the winter, there

The captains organized races and games with the Nez Perce. This woodcut shows young Native American boys about to start a horse race.

were enough horses for each person to ride one and to use as packhorses or for food.

To keep the men in condition after their month of rest, the captains organized games and footraces with the Nez Perce. All the while, the camas plants were bursting into bloom on the Weippe Prairie, so that the corps lived and worked in a waving sea of blue flowers. Everyone wished that they could stay in this beautiful, abundant place forever instead of crossing the jagged peaks looming just ahead of them.

Over the Mountains—Again

It was June, and the Corps of Discovery was now ready to start its trek over the mountains. The Nez Perce warned the captains that if they attempted to cross the Bitterroot Range before July 1, their horses would have to go for three days without food at the summit, as there would not be enough grass for them there. But Lewis and Clark were anxious to return home. The crew was rested, they had gathered plenty of food, the weather was perfect—it was time to go!

On Sunday, June 15, the corps began the journey back over the Rockies. Up and up they traveled, sometimes riding horseback, sometimes walking to let the horses rest. Baptiste was almost too big for his cradleboard by now but he had to ride in it on his mother's saddle, as he had done since he was a tiny baby.

The crew was rested, they had gathered plenty of food, the weather was perfect—it was time to go!

The nights became colder, and the wildflowers gave way to pine forests. Whenever the group passed a meadow of grass, they stopped to let the horses eat their fill. But the snow was growing ominously deep, and after only a few days, the group was struggling in snow twelve to fifteen feet deep. The captains decided they would have to retreat temporarily and make another attempt after the snow melted further.

Surely the captains felt ashamed for ignoring the Nez Perce advice. They ordered the group to quickly bury some unneeded gear and stash the rest in the trees away from animals. Then, as fast as they could, the corps retreated back down the mountains—all the way to the Weippe Prairie once more.

On June 24, the corps returned to the mountains, this time bringing three Nez Perce guides who agreed to come along as far as the Great Falls. Even though it had only been a week since their first attempt, the snow had already melted enough for the horses to paw their way through to grass. With the help of the guides, warming weather, and plenty of food and horses, the corps made an uneventful crossing.

By July 3, the corps had passed just beyond the Bitterroot Range. The captains ordered a break at a creek they called

Traveler's Rest, so that the group could do laundry, hunt, and graze the horses. Lewis and Clark decided they could perhaps make better use of their time if they split the corps into two groups from here on out. Each captain would lead a group and explore areas unseen on the outward journey.

After much discussion, they decided that Clark would take a group including Charbonneau and Sacagawea south through the mountains until they reached Three Forks. From there, they would head east to the Yellowstone River. Sacagawea and Charbonneau's interpreting skills could come in handy should they encounter the Crow tribe, whose language was very similar to Hidatsa. Lewis's group would travel to the Great Falls and then explore the area north of the Missouri River. The entire corps would reunite at the junction of the Yellowstone and Missouri rivers.

The captains knew this was a sound plan, but there was still cause for concern. This would be the first time the Corps of Discovery would be separated for an extended length of time. They had been extraordinarily lucky so far, but who knew when that luck might run out? They could only hope they would see each other alive again.

Guiding Clark's Group

As Sacagawea and Clark's group traveled south through the plains and mountains, they passed nearby the familiar land of Sacagawea's childhood. She recognized the landmarks and trails and showed Clark the best, most direct routes to take. At one point, the corps was following a well-traveled tribal road when it came out onto a plain and lost the trail. But Sacagawea knew this place, she told Clark. She had gathered roots here many times as a child. That gap in the mountains was the pass that would lead them to Camp Fortunate, near the Jefferson River. There they would find the canoes they had sunk the previous summer near the Shoshone camp in preparation for the Rockies crossing.

Clark must have known by now that Sacagawea could be trusted. He obeyed her instructions, and the crew found the canoes and the gear they had buried in underground caches. To their delight, everything was in almost-perfect condition. Even the chewing tobacco they had buried was still there.

As Sacagawea and Clark's group traveled south through the plains and mountains, they passed nearby the familiar land of Sacagawea's childhood.

By July 13, Clark's crew had subdivided, with one party taking the canoes down the Jefferson River (one of the three forks) to the Great Falls. This group was transporting most of the gear to the meeting spot with Lewis. Clark, Sacagawea, Charbonneau, and eight others rode horseback overland to the Yellowstone River. The group found themselves facing a mountain range, with two roads leading through two passes.

Clark thought the northerly pass might be the one to lead to the Yellowstone, even though it was twenty miles out of the way. Sacagawea told him that she knew this land, too, and that the southern pass was by far the best way to reach the river. She was correct again, and that route, known today as the Bozeman Pass, is still the best way to travel that section of the Rockies. One day, many decades in the future, the Northern Pacific Railway would be built on that very road.

When they reached the Yellowstone on July 15, Clark sent a small party overland with the horses and some gear, while he and the others built small hide-covered canoes, so that they could ride the current of the Yellowstone downstream to the meeting place with Lewis.

This c. 1904 painting by Alfred Russell depicts Sacagawea pointing the correct way to go.

In the course of their journey across the plains, the group encountered a very strange-looking rock looming up from the land near present-day Billings, Montana. This natural pillar was about two hundred feet high and sheer on all sides but one. That one side could be climbed, and for centuries, local tribes had carved art and figures all over the stone. Clark carved this inscription: "Wm Clark July 25th 1806." Before the group left, Clark named the rock "Pompy's Pillar." "Pompy" was his nickname for little Jean-Baptiste. Later, when expedition member Nicholas Biddle wrote his own version of the journey, he changed the name to "Pompey's Pillar," after the Roman general who was killed after challenging Julius Caesar.

On August 2, Clark's party reached the junction of the Yellowstone and Missouri rivers. They had made it! Now all they had to do was rest, hunt, and wait for Lewis and the rest of the corps to catch up.

Clark named this rock formation near Billings, Montana, "Pompy's Pillar" in honor of Sacagawea's little boy.

However, that night, swarms of mosquitoes attacked them, biting them so much that little Baptiste's face swelled up. The swarm continued unabated for four days. No one could function—they couldn't hunt, dress skins, dry meat, or sleep. When Clark tried to shoot an elk, his gun misfired from the mosquitoes jamming the barrel.

Finally, Clark decided that they had to move on. He wrote a note for Lewis and stuck it on the pole at the river junction. As quickly as they could, the group packed their gear and moved down the river. But the pests continued biting until finally, the weather changed and cold wind swept the insects away.

On August 12, they were reunited with the rest of the corps downriver from the junction of the Yellowstone and Missouri rivers. Lewis was suffering from a bullet wound in his buttock after Pierre Cruzatte, who was partially blind, had mistaken him for an elk and shot the captain while hunting. Otherwise, all were well—and eager to continue. They were only five days from Fort Mandan!

CHAPTER 13

Journey's End

[Sacagawea] was particularly useful among the Shoshones. Indeed, she has borne with patience truly admirable the fatigues of so long a route encumbered with the charge of an infant.

—*William Clark*

It is easy to imagine Sacagawea heaving a great sigh of relief as the corps entered the Hidatsa and Mandan villages on August 15, 1806—one year and four months after setting out from that very spot. She had traveled through the untamed Rockies twice and was reunited with her native Shoshone tribe. She had visited the Pacific Ocean and had seen the skeleton of a great whale. This brave young woman had survived serious illness and near drowning, and now, here she was—healthy, strong, and with the bright-eyed, crowing Baptiste still strapped to her back.

At the villages, corps members scattered for different parts. Some members decided to strike out on their own for other trading posts. Others stayed with Lewis and Clark and accompanied them on the rest of the journey down the Missouri to St. Louis. Charbonneau decided to stay in the Hidatsa village with Sacagawea and the baby, despite the captains' invitation to come with them to St. Louis. Perhaps Sacagawea pressured her husband to remain, so that they could rest among their own tribe. Or perhaps Charbonneau

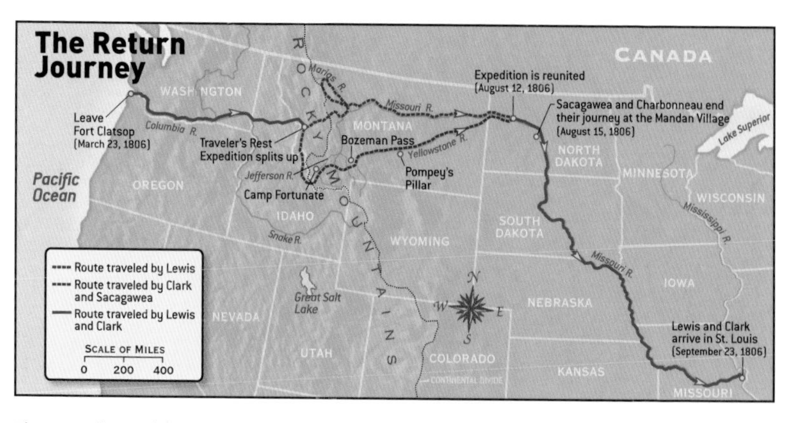

This map shows the corps's route after leaving Fort Clatsop and splitting up at Traveler's Rest. Sacagawea and Charbonneau left the corps soon after the groups reunited on August 12.

thought his chances for trading would be better among the Mandan. Either way, Charbonneau was paid his wages of $500.33. Sacagawea, despite the captains' repeated praise and obvious admiration for her, was paid nothing.

Clark's Offer

Throughout all of these preparations, Clark was doing some serious thinking of his own. He had become very attached to Sacagawea, and especially little Baptiste, throughout their long days together. His heart wrenched at the thought of leaving the baby behind, perhaps never to see him again. So Clark made an offer to Charbonneau and Sacagawea. He offered to adopt Baptiste, whom he called "a [beautiful] promising child," and take him to St. Louis. There, Clark promised to give the young boy the best kind of upbringing and to provide him with the highest quality education. Clark assumed, as many would have, that this life would be better for the boy than traveling the country or living in a Hidatsa village with his Indian mother and fur-trader father.

But Sacagawea and her husband shook their heads. The baby was too young to leave his mother, they pointed out. He was not yet **weaned**. In one year, they told Clark, he would be old enough, and then they would bring him to St. Louis for Clark to adopt.

Clark reluctantly agreed to wait a year, but a few days after he and Lewis left the village and began their paddle down the Missouri, he wrote Sacagawea and Charbonneau a letter that laid his heart on the page. He strongly urged them, he wrote, to reconsider their decision and to come immediately to St. Louis. If they came, he would give Charbonneau a piece of land in his possession, along with some horses, cows, and hogs. They could farm the land while Clark took charge of Baptiste's education. Or, Clark wrote, he could get Charbonneau an interpreter position with the army—which would soon be sending troops to the Mandan and Hidatsa villages. If Sacagawea and her husband could deliver Pompy to St. Louis, they could then travel back up the river with the soldiers.

Another proposition suggested that if Charbonneau wanted to return to his old freelance trading position, Clark would help him acquire merchandise to start out with or even go into partnership with him on a small boat of trade goods. No matter what Charbonneau decided, Clark wrote that it would be best if Sacagawea came

William Clark, shown in this modern drawing, offered to adopt Sacagawea's son, Baptiste.

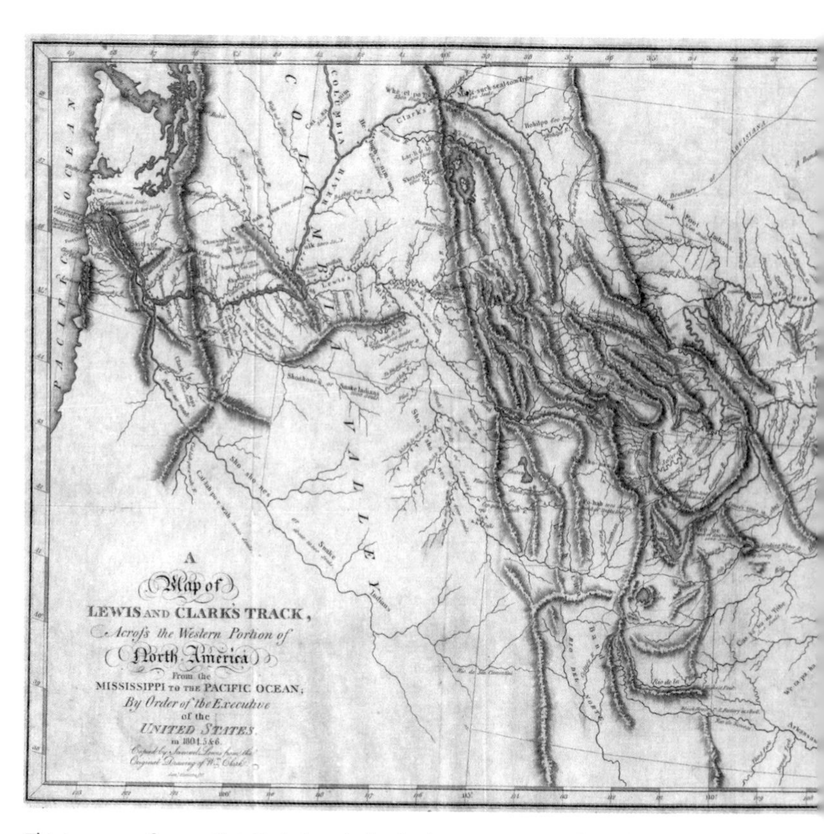

This is a copy of a map that Clark drew. It details the corps's journey from the Mississippi River to the Pacific Ocean.

with the baby and stayed with him until Baptiste was a little older. Already missing his surrogate family, Clark probably sent the letter back upstream with a passing canoe, in hopes that Charbonneau and Sacagawea would read it and respond. There is no record of response by Charbonneau or Sacagawea, but the likelihood is that they received the letter, because a few years later, they did indeed take Baptiste to St. Louis and accept Clark's offer of help.

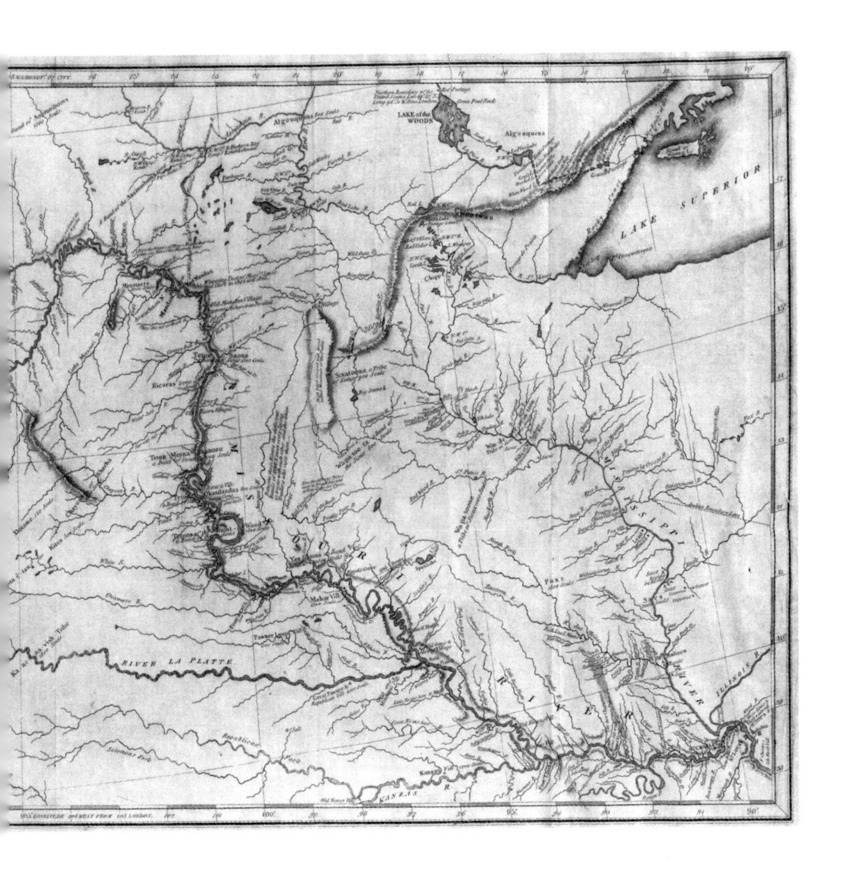

Lewis and Clark reached St. Louis on September 23, 1806. They had traveled 7,689 miles, and by all accounts the expedition had been a tremendous success. Though they had not found the Northwest Passage, they had mapped a vast swath of the country, established relations with hundreds of Native American tribes, and found a route, albeit an arduous one, to the Pacific.

A New Life in St. Louis

History left no record of Sacagawea's activities from 1806 until 1809. Presumably, she and Charbonneau remained in the

When Sacagawea arrived in St. Louis, Missouri, in 1809, she may have seen this idyllic settlement on Chouteau's Pond.

Hidatsa village, working and raising Baptiste. They had not forgotten their promise to Clark, however, and in the fall of 1809, the little family arrived in the bustling frontier town that was St. Louis. They immediately wrote to Clark, indicating that they would have come sooner, but tribal warfare south of the Mandan village had made traveling impossible.

There is no record of Sacagawea's impression of St. Louis, but it was by far the largest, and perhaps the only town she had ever seen. Though St. Louis in those days was mostly a collection of log cabins and muddy roads clustered on the banks of the Missouri River, the crowds and noise must have been overwhelming.

Clark was not in the city, however, having left two months earlier on a business trip to Washington. A friend of his, Auguste Chocteau, was put in touch with the family, and it was he who was present on December 28, 1809, when little Baptiste was baptized in a log cabin church. A monk named Father Urban Guillet, wearing a white robe, touched the water onto the little boy's forehead and murmured the prayers as Charbonneau, Sacagawea, and Chocteau looked on. Since Clark was not present, Chocteau was named as godfather to Baptiste.

Clark returned to the city that summer, and in the fall of 1810 helped Charbonneau buy a parcel of land to farm, as he had promised years before. At some point, he also replaced Chocteau as Baptiste's godfather. For reasons unknown, farming did not agree with Charbonneau, and perhaps, with Sacagawea. It seems that they felt stifled in the city, and Sacagawea became ill. She was also homesick for Shoshone land. So, on March 26, 1811, Charbonneau sold the land back to Clark for one hundred dollars, and bought fifty pounds of hardtack, a hard biscuit used as food when traveling. He and Sacagawea had put their names down as members of fur trader Manuel Lisa's newest expedition, which was traveling back up the Missouri to Three Forks. Baptiste would remain with Clark, who was now his godfather, in St. Louis.

When Charbonneau and Sacagawea left St. Louis, did they mean to leave forever? Or did they think they would return to see their son in a few months—or a few years? There is no way of knowing. But the couple had made up their minds and on April 2, 1811, Sacagawea kissed her son, handed him to Clark, and departed with Lisa's expedition.

On that first day, a journalist who was accompanying the group recorded, "We have on board a Frenchman named Charbonet [Charbonneau], with his wife, an Indian woman of the Snake [Shoshone] nation, both of whom accompanied Lewis and Clark to the Pacific, and were of great service. The woman, a good creature, of a mild and gentle disposition, was greatly attached to the whites, whose manners and airs she tries to imitate; but she had become sickly and longed to revisit her native country; her husband also, who had spent many years amongst the Indians, was become weary of civilized life."

Manuel Lisa's Fort

Lisa pushed his group to travel quickly. A larger group was ahead of them and catching up would mean greater protection against hostile tribes along the way. For a month, the men worked

The North American Fur Trade

By the time of Lewis and Clark's expedition, the fur trade was already firmly established in North America. Since the 1500s, Europeans had been trading furs with Native American tribes. They would send these furs back to Europe, where they would be made into hats and other goods. Beaver was the most valuable fur since hats made out of it were in high demand. Lewis and Clark opened up trading contacts with many tribes and then traders like Manuel Lisa followed them in later years, establishing trading centers all through the United States and Canada.

But starting in the 1700s, the fur trade began to decline. As more and more settlers moved into North America and began clearing land for farming, animals became harder and harder to find. Some animals, like the beaver, had also been over-trapped. But the real blow to the fur trade came in the 1830s, when European hatmakers began using silk for their hats instead of beaver fur. By the 1870s, most fur trade had ceased.

The popular beaver hat, shown here, that created demand for beaver fur came to an end when hatmakers started using silk.

Sacagawea and Charbonneau resumed their life in the Mandan village and probably stayed in an earthen hut similar to the one shown here.

long days, towing and rowing the boats upstream. Finally, in June of 1811, the expedition, including Sacagawea and Charbonneau, reached the Hidatsa and Mandan villages. Here, Sacagawea and Charbonneau rested for the winter, probably staying in their old hut among their adopted tribe. It is likely that Sacagawea was ill during this time, and perhaps tired of traveling. She may have just wanted to see her native land and rest there among her tribe. But this was not to be her future.

Lisa's expedition pushed on and reached the Three Forks region sometime after the winter of 1811–1812. But the group did not even get near the Three Forks camping grounds because the hostile Blackfeet tribe kept everyone away. Instead, the trading group was forced to travel on, and Sacagawea did not see her Shoshone people. Finally the expedition reached a bluff seventy miles south of present-day Bismarck, North Dakota. Here they settled down for the winter and built a fort, completing it on November 19.

Earlier on the journey, sometime in August, Sacagawea had given birth to a little girl, and named her Lizette. She surely tried to care for the baby as best as she could, but the mother was growing sicker, and perhaps was weakened from the birth.

To make matters worse, Lisa's fort was plagued with problems almost from the beginning. The trappers and traders were fighting among one another, tired, perhaps, of the cold weather and ice-choked river. The tribes in the area were also fighting one another, adding to the already tense atmosphere, and some tribe members had started breaking into the fort and stealing valuable items like tools and horses. The prairie wind whistled through the walls unceasingly. Three of Lisa's men were found dead, killed by a local tribe.

Earlier on the journey, sometime in August, Sacagawea had given birth to a little girl, and named her Lizette.

A Lonely Death

It was in this chaotic, violent atmosphere that Sacagawea lay dying on Sunday, December 20. No one really knows what was wrong with her. She may have had typhoid fever, with its symptoms of chills, fever, vomiting, and diarrhea. Whatever was wrong with her, there is little doubt that her dying was lonely. She was far from her native tribe and her adopted one. Charbonneau may or may not have been there, but he had been away from the fort on trading trips most of the winter. Lewis, with his medical skill, was not there to attend her this time. One can imagine her, lying on a hard makeshift bed in a corner, perhaps occasionally offered water, but for the most part, ignored.

That evening, a clerk at the fort, John Luttig, made some inconsequential entries into his journal, including: "[T]his evening the Wife of Charbonneau a Snake Squaw, died of putrid fever[.]

[S]he was a good and the best Women in the fort, aged about 25 year[s.] [S]he left a fine infant girl."

Another Ending

Sacagawea's death seems clear-cut, but for some historians, history is a great deal more muddy. Citing oral histories obtained from elderly Shoshone who claimed to have known Sacagawea, these scholars have put forth an alternate version of Sacagawea's life after the expedition. They allege that she did not die at Manuel Lisa's trading post, leaving behind a little daughter. In fact, these historians believe that Sacagawea never went on this journey at all. They maintain it was Charbonneau's long-forgotten other wife, Otter Woman, who accompanied him to Lisa's trading post and died at a young age. Perhaps Otter Woman claimed some of Sacagawea's accomplishments as her own and bragged about having been with Lewis and Clark to the Pacific Ocean.

The *real* Sacagawea, according to this theory, lived for many, many more years, traveling all over the country and living with many tribes as a sort of nomad. This Sacagawea had another son, named Bazil, and eventually married a Comanche named Jerk Meat. While she was living with the Comanches, she took the name Porivo.

The real *Sacagawea, according to this theory, lived for many, many more years, traveling . . . and living with many tribes as a sort of nomad.*

Eventually, the story goes, following the death of her husband, Porivo made her way to the Wind River Reservation in Wyoming, where she finally settled down with her son Bazil among her native Shoshone. She became rather

A gravestone for Sacagawea stands in a Shoshone cemetery in Fort Washakie, Wyoming.

famous among the white people she met, all of whom knew she had been on an expedition with white men. This Native American woman died a peaceful, happy death in 1884, lovingly surrounded by her family and tribe.

Sacagawea's Legacy

For most of the nineteenth century, Sacagawea was an unknown, unheralded figure. Her story was revived in a 1902 novel, *The Conquest: The True Story of Lewis and Clark*, by Eva Emery Dye, who is responsible for much of modern society's view of the young woman. Dye wove a fictional narrative that transformed Sacagawea into a Native American princess (based on the fact that her brother, Cameahwait, was a chief). It perpetuated the myth that named Sacagawea as the guide of the Lewis and Clark expedition and created a romance out of her relationship with Clark. A very compelling story indeed—but almost entirely untrue.

Eva Emery Dye was the author who brought the story of Sacagawea to the public's attention.

Sacagawea was not a Shoshone princess in any sense of the word, though her family may have had high status in the tribe. She was certainly *not* the guide of the expedition. She was able to point the way through areas she was familiar with, but in unfamiliar terrain, she was as lost as any corps member. And there is no historical evidence of a romantic relationship between Sacagawea and Clark.

Because of these myths, it is hard to accept Sacagawea for what she really was: an extraordinarily tough, brave, and resourceful person who lived through an incredible journey at a very young age. Sacagawea endured everything the men endured while constantly having to care for an infant. More than that, she collected much-needed food along the way and proved to be an invaluable interpreter. She also served as a peace symbol, defusing many potential conflicts on the journey. Through it all, she was an uncomplaining and kind person. By all accounts, this unassuming Native American teenager contributed a great deal of strength and resourcefulness to one of the great expeditions in American history.

In honor of Sacagawea and her contribution to the opening of the West, the U.S. Mint immortalized her on a Golden Dollar coin in the year 2000.

Glossary

abscess—a collection of pus in the body, with swelling and inflammation.

caches—hiding places, dug in the ground, used for storing provisions or valuables.

camas—a plant in the lily family that has blue flowers and a bulb-like root, used as an important food source by many Native American tribes.

cannibalism—the eating of human flesh by another human.

conquistadores—the Spanish conquerors of Mexico and Peru in the sixteenth century.

corps—a military organization of officers and enlisted soldiers.

council—a meeting called for consultation, deliberation, or discussion.

credit—confidence in a purchaser's intention and ability to pay, displayed by entrusting the buyer with goods without immediate payment.

emissary—a representative sent on a mission or errand.

helm—the wheel or tiller by which a boat is steered.

miscarriage—discharge of the fetus from the womb before it is ready to be born.

mumps—an infectious disease that usually involves the swelling of the salivary glands.

phonetically—corresponding to the way a word sounds when spoken.

platonic—a relationship that does not involve romantic desire.

portage—to carry boats overland from one water route to another.

poultice—a soft, moist mass of cloth, bread, herbs, or other substances applied hot to an area of the body, and meant to warm and heal that area.

saltworks—a place where salt is made.

seminomadic—a term describing people who primarily move from place to place throughout the year but who may plant some crops at one point or remain at a certain place for an extended period of time.

suet—a hard, fatty tissue of cattle, bison, and sheep.

travois—transporting devices made of a frame joined by two poles and pulled by a horse or a dog.

weaned—having accustomed a child to food other than his or her mother's milk.

Bibliography

Books

Barbie, Donna. "Sacagawea: The Making of a Myth." *Sifters: Native American Women's Lives*. Ed. Theda Perdue. Oxford, UK: Oxford University Press, 2001. 60–76.

Bowers, Alfred W. *Mandan Social and Ceremonial Organization*. Chicago: University of Chicago Press, 1950.

Clark, Ella E. and Margot Edmonds. *Sacagawea of the Lewis and Clark Expedition*. Berkeley, CA: University of California Press, 1979.

Colby, Susan M. *Sacagawea's Child: The Life and Times of Jean-Baptiste (Pomp) Charbonneau*. Spokane, WA: The Arthur H. Clark Company, 2005.

DeVoto, Bernard, ed. *The Journals of Lewis and Clark*. New York: Houghton Mifflin, 1953.

Foley, William E. *Wilderness Journey: The Life of William Clark*. Columbia, MO: University of Missouri Press, 2004.

Howard, Harold P. *Sacajawea*. Norman, OK: University of Oklahoma Press, 1971.

Karttunen, Frances. *Between Worlds: Interpreters, Guides, and Survivors*. New Brunswick, NJ: Rutgers University Press, 2004.

Lowry, Thomas P. *Venereal Disease and the Lewis and Clark Expedition*. Lincoln, NE: University of Nebraska Press, 2004.

Mann, John W.W. *Sacajawea's People: The Lemhi Shoshones and the Salmon River Country*. Lincoln, NE: University of Nebraska Press, 2004.

Matthews, Washington. *Ethnography and Philology of the Hidatsa Indians*. Washington, DC: Government Printing Office, 1877.

McCall, Laura. "Sacagawea: A Historical Enigma." *Ordinary Women, Extraordinary Lives: Women in American History*. Ed. Kriste Lindenmeyer. Wilmington, DE: Scholarly Resources Books, 2000. 39–54.

Morris, Larry E. *The Fate of the Corps: What Became of the Lewis and Clark Explorers After the Expedition*. New Haven, CT: Yale University Press, 2004.

Nash, Alice and Christoph Strobel. *Daily Life of Native Americans From Post-Columbian Through Nineteenth Century America*. Westport, CT: Greenwood Press, 2006.

Nelson, W. Dale. *Interpreters with Lewis and Clark: The Story of Sacagawea and Toussaint Charbonneau*. Denton, TX: University of North Texas Press, 2003.

Slaughter, Thomas P. *Exploring Lewis and Clark: Reflections on Men and Wilderness*. New York: Alfred A. Knopf, 2003.

Articles

Lawrence, Jenny, "In Their Own Words," *Natural History*, August 1991.

Mathes, Valerie Shirer, "A New Look at the Role of Women in Indian Society," *American Indian Quarterly*, Summer 1975.

Web Sites

Daniels, Martha, "Traveling on the Wild Missouri River," *Outside In Online*, 2008, http://mdc.mo.gov/kids/out-in/2003/01/2.htm.

"The Fur Trade," Powell County Museum and Arts Foundation, 2008, http://www.pcmaf.org/fur_trade.htm.

"Northwest Passage," Encyclopedia Britannica Online, http://www.britannica.com/EBchecked/topic/420084/Northwest-Passage.

Interviews

Hammond, Jeff (Master Instructor, Northwest Boat School), interview by Emma Carlson Berne, August 27, 2008.

Source Notes

The following citations list the sources of quoted material in this book. The first and last few words of each quotation are cited and followed by their source. Complete information on referenced sources can be found in the Bibliography.

Abbreviations:

ILC—*Interpreters with Lewis and Clark*

ITOW—"In Their Own Words," *Natural History*

SLCE—*Sacagawea of the Lewis and Clark Expedition*

TFC—*The Fate of the Corps*

TJLC—*The Journals of Lewis and Clark*

Note: DeVoto's book is a compilation of journals written by Meriwether Lewis, William Clark, and Nicholas Biddle. The words in quotes are not DeVoto's, but those of Lewis, Clark, and Biddle.

WJ—*Wilderness Journey*

INTRODUCTION: The Land of Her Birth

PAGE 1 "*[The] Indian woman . . . retreat of her nation. . . .*": TJLC, p. 181

CHAPTER 1: A Shoshone Girl, a Hidatsa Captive

PAGE 2 "*[She] assures us that . . . of [its] source.*": TJLC, p. 181

CHAPTER 2: Life among the Hidatsa

PAGE 13 "*[Two squaws] . . . frenchmen came down[.]*": TJLC, p. 64

CHAPTER 3: The Corps of Discovery

PAGE 19 "*[Y]our mission is . . . across this continent.*": TJLC, p. xv

PAGE 22 "*The object of your . . . purposes of commerce.*": TJLC, p. xv

PAGE 24 "*good hunters, stout . . . pretty considerable degree.*": WJ, p. 58

CHAPTER 4: Joining the Expedition

PAGE 28 "*[A] French man name[d] . . . the Snake language.*": WJ, p. 96

PAGE 30 "*[A] French man name[d] . . . the Snake language.*": WJ, p. 96

CHAPTER 5: Birth and Unrest at Fort Mandan

PAGE 34 "*[O]ur interpreter . . . mentioned yesterday.*": TJLC p. 85

PAGE 35 "*[A]bout five oClock . . . the pain violent.*": TJLC, p. 80

CHAPTER 6: The Journey Begins

PAGE 43 "*The Indian woman . . . were washed overboard.*": TJLC, p. 111

PAGE 51 "*the Indian woman . . . were washed overboard.*": TJLC, p. 111

PAGE 51 "*this stream we called . . . the Snake woman.*": TJLC, p. 113

CHAPTER 7: Near Death and Danger

PAGE 52 *"[The] Indian woman. . . . some what dangerous."*: TJLC, p. 141

PAGE 55 *"if She dies . . . am now convinced."*: WJ, p. 111

PAGE 57 *"the grandest sight. . . . grand [scenery]."*: TJLC, pp. 137–138

PAGE 58 *"[tearing] up everything before it,"*: TJLC, p. 152

CHAPTER 8: In Shoshone Country

PAGE 60 *"I cannot discover . . . perfectly content anywhere."*: ILC, p. 36

PAGE 61 *"I cannot discover . . . perfectly content anywhere."*: ILC, p. 36

CHAPTER 9: A Homecoming

PAGE 66 *"[Clark] saw [Sacagawea] . . . her native tribe."*: TJLC, p. 202

PAGE 66 *"I was heartily . . . the national hug."*: TJLC, p. 191

PAGE 68 *"when we arrived . . . had not yet arrived."*: TJLC, p. 200

PAGE 69 *"I mentioned to . . . I could do signs."*: TJLC, p. 201

PAGE 70 *"embraced with the. . . . interest of their situation."*: TJLC, p. 203

CHAPTER 10: Crossing the Rocky Mountains

PAGE 76 *"[As] Soon as they. . . . our friendly intentions."*: TJLC, pp. 256–257

PAGE 78 *"the most terrible . . . I ever beheld."*: ILC, p. 44

CHAPTER 11: A Winter in the Rain

PAGE 85 *"She had traveled. . . . permitted to See either."*: ILC, p. 51

PAGE 91 *"She had traveled. . . . permitted to See either."*: ILC, p. 51

CHAPTER 12: Eastward Bound

PAGE 94 *"The [I]ndian woman . . . which I shall cross."*: SLCE, p. 74

CHAPTER 13: Journey's End

PAGE 105 *"[Sacagawea] was. . . . charge of an infant."*: SLCE, p. 82

PAGE 106 *"a [beautiful] promising child"*: TJLC, p. 458

PAGE 111 *"We have on board. . . . weary of civilized life."*: TFC, p. 107

PAGE 115 *"[T]his evening. . . . a fine infant girl."*: TFC, p.115

Image Credits

© North Wind Picture Archives/Alamy: 20
Brennan Dalsgard Publishers/Madame Talbot: 56 (top)
Karen Carr: 28
Karen Carr/Illinois Historic Preservation Agency/Lewis and Clark State Historic Site: 107
© CORBIS: 3, 12, 21
© Academy of Natural Sciences of Philadelphia/CORBIS: 14
© Bettmann/CORBIS: 5, 26, 103
© Macduff Everton/CORBIS: 57
© Fine Art Photographic Library/CORBIS: 59
© Historical Picture Archive/CORBIS: 54

© The Mariners' Museum/CORBIS: 82
© Connie Ricca/CORBIS: 81
Elizabeth Beard/winninator/www.flickr.com: 113
Merritt Brown/Crick3/www.flickr.com: 116
Ken Cobb/www.flickr.com: 104
Gary Conner/www.flickr.com: 2
John DeGraff/www.flickr.com: 27, 64
Anne Elliott/www.flickr.com: 48 (bottom)
Beverly Hoeftman, Greenbelt, MD/www.flickr.com: 51
Laureen LaBar/lwww.flickr.com: 61
Rogier Mulder/rheauchyr/www.flickr.com: 38
Robert M. Mutch/www.flickr.com: 80
Thomas W. Schoeller/SaddleTramp Images/www.flickr.com: 78
Glenn Scofield Williams/www.flickr.com: 93
Cliff Zener/www.flickr.com: 92
Karen Montgomery/www.flickr.com: 42
Fort Mandan Foundation: 95
The Granger Collection, New York: 8, 16, 31, 39, 67, 84, 90, 112
Michael Haynes: 23 (left and right), 24, 32, 33, 35 (bottom), 37, 44, 46, 53, 68, 71, 88
Independence National Historical Park: 19
© iStockphoto.com/"John Bell": 35 (top)
© iStockphoto.com/"SlidePix": 48 (top)
Library of Congress: 7, 9, 10, 11, 25, 36, 47, 62, 72, 77, 86, 96, 108–109
Map by Jim McMahon: 106
© North Wind/North Wind Picture Archives: 6, 99, 110
Oregon Historical Society Research Library: 117 (top)
Courtesy of Pennsylvania Hospital Historic Collections, Philadelphia: 97
Ron Ukrainetz: 17, 56 (bottom)
U.S. Army: 83
The United States Mint: 117 (bottom)
Cover art: Michael Haynes

About the Author

Emma Carlson Berne has written and edited over two dozen books for children and young adults, including biographies of such diverse subjects as Shakespeare, Frida Kahlo, Snoop Dogg, and Christopher Columbus. She lives in Cincinnati, Ohio.

Index